THE FACEBOOK MARKETING SECRETS GUIDE

The steps and strategies, technique to follow

Kane Schiller

Copyright

© [2024] by All rights reserved.
No part of this publication may be reproduced, distributed, or transmitted in any form or by any means, including photocopying, recording, or other electronic or mechanical methods, without the prior written permission of the publisher, except in the case of brief quotations embodied in critical reviews and certain other noncommercial uses permitted by copyright law.

Table of Contents

Copyright   1
Table of Contents   2
Introduction   4
Introduction   9
    Why Facebook? Understanding Its Power and Reach   12
    How to Use This Guide for Maximum Results   16
Chapter 1: Building Your Facebook Marketing Foundation   21
    Setting Up Your Business Page: A Step-by-Step Guide   25
    Defining Your Marketing Goals   28
    Identifying and Understanding Your Target Audience   32
    Crafting a Compelling Brand Story   37
Chapter 2: Content Creation and Engagement Strategies   42
    Creating Content That Captivates   48
    The Art of Storytelling on Facebook   54
    Utilizing Visuals: Photos, Videos, and Live Streams   60
    Engaging with Your Audience: Comments, Messages, and Community Building   66
Chapter 3: Mastering Facebook Advertising   73
    Introduction to Facebook Ads   81
    Crafting Irresistible Ad Copy   89
    Choosing the Right Ad Format for Your Goals   98

Advanced Targeting Techniques: Custom
Audiences and Lookalikes   106
A/B Testing and Optimizing Your Ads   114

Chapter 4: Analytics and Performance Tracking 122
Understanding Facebook Insights   130
Key Metrics to Monitor   140
Using Data to Improve Your Strategy   143
Reporting and Presenting Results   146

Chapter 5: Advanced Strategies for Facebook Success   **151**
Leveraging Facebook Groups for Engagement 158
Influencer Partnerships and Collaborations   165
Running Contests and Giveaways   171
Integrating Facebook with Other Marketing
Channels   178
Staying Ahead of Facebook Algorithm Changes 185

Appendix   **192**
Glossary of Facebook Marketing Terms   201
Resources and Tools for Facebook Marketers 208
Template: Facebook Marketing Plan   212

Conclusion   **218**

Introduction

Michael had always dreamt of running a successful online business. He poured his heart into creating high-quality, unique products that he was sure people would love. He built a sleek, user-friendly website, took professional photos of his products, and wrote compelling descriptions. However, despite his best efforts, the sales just weren't coming in.

Day after day, Michael would check his sales dashboard, only to see the same disheartening zero. He tried everything he could think of—promotions, discounts, even free shipping—but nothing seemed to work. His frustration grew as he watched his savings dwindle away. The reality was harsh: if he couldn't figure out how to sell his products, his dream of running a successful business would be over before it even began.

One evening, while browsing through an online forum for small business owners, Michael stumbled upon a post about a book titled "The Facebook

Marketing Secrets Guide." The post was filled with success stories from entrepreneurs who had turned their businesses around using strategies from the book. Skeptical but desperate, Michael decided to give it a shot. He ordered the book and waited anxiously for it to arrive.

When the book finally landed on his doorstep, Michael tore open the package and began reading. The guide was packed with detailed, actionable advice on how to leverage Facebook's powerful marketing tools. It covered everything from setting up a business page, creating engaging content, targeting specific audiences, to running effective ad campaigns. Michael was particularly intrigued by the case studies that showed real-world examples of businesses that had skyrocketed their sales using these strategies.

With renewed hope, Michael decided to put the book's advice into practice. He started by revamping his Facebook business page, ensuring it was visually appealing and clearly communicated his brand's message. He then began posting regular content that was not only promotional but also engaging and informative, aiming to build a community around his brand.

The next step was to dive into Facebook's ad platform. Michael used the guide to learn how to create targeted ads that would reach potential customers who were most likely to be interested in his products. He set a modest budget for his first campaign, choosing to focus on a specific demographic that matched his ideal customer profile.

The results were almost immediate. Within a few days, Michael began to see an uptick in traffic to his website. People were liking and sharing his posts, and more importantly, they were buying his products. The zero on his sales dashboard was finally replaced by numbers that steadily climbed each day.

Encouraged by his initial success, Michael continued to refine his Facebook marketing strategy. He experimented with different types of ads, used A/B testing to see what resonated most with his audience, and kept a close eye on the analytics to track his progress. He also engaged with his followers, responding to comments and messages, which helped build a loyal customer base.

Over the next few months, Michael's business transformed. His products were flying off the virtual shelves, and his brand was gaining recognition. The book that had once been his last hope had turned into his secret weapon. Michael's hard work, combined with the insights from "The Facebook Marketing Secrets Guide," had finally paid off.

Michael's story became an inspiration for other struggling entrepreneurs. He often shared his journey and the lessons he had learned, encouraging others to not give up and to seek out the knowledge and tools they needed to succeed. His success was a testament to the power of perseverance, smart marketing, and the right guidance.

In the end, Michael's business not only survived but thrived, all thanks to a chance encounter with a book that unlocked the secrets to effective Facebook marketing.

Introduction

Welcome to the World of Facebook Marketing

In today's digital age, having a robust online presence is no longer optional for businesses; it's essential. Among the myriad social media platforms available, Facebook stands out as a powerhouse, boasting over 2.8 billion monthly active users. It's not just a platform for connecting with friends and family; it's a dynamic space where businesses can engage with customers, build brand loyalty, and drive sales. Whether you're a small business owner, a marketer, or an entrepreneur, mastering Facebook marketing is crucial to your success.

Why Facebook? Understanding Its Power and Reach

Facebook's vast reach and advanced targeting capabilities make it an unparalleled tool for marketers. Unlike other platforms, Facebook allows you to pinpoint your ideal audience based on demographics, interests, and behaviors. This precision targeting ensures that your marketing efforts are not just wide-reaching but also highly effective. From brand awareness campaigns to driving direct sales, Facebook offers a range of tools and features to help you achieve your business goals.

But why is Facebook so powerful? Here are a few key reasons:

1. Global Audience: With users from every corner of the globe, Facebook provides an unparalleled platform to reach diverse audiences.

2. Engagement Opportunities: From posts and stories to ads and live streams, Facebook offers numerous ways to engage with your audience.

3. Data-Driven Insights: Facebook's analytics tools provide deep insights into your audience's behaviors and preferences, allowing you to refine your strategies continuously.

4. Cost-Effective Advertising: Compared to traditional advertising methods, Facebook ads offer a high return on investment, making it accessible for businesses of all sizes.

How to Use This Guide for Maximum Results

"The Facebook Marketing Secrets Guide" is designed to be your comprehensive companion on the journey to Facebook marketing mastery. Whether you're starting from scratch or looking to enhance your existing efforts, this guide provides step-by-step instructions, expert tips, and real-life examples to ensure your success. Here's how to make the most of this guide:

1. Follow the Chapters Sequentially: Each chapter builds on the previous one, ensuring you develop a strong foundation before moving on to more advanced topics.

2. Apply What You Learn: Don't just read through the strategies and techniques—apply them to your own Facebook marketing efforts. Experiment, analyze, and adjust your tactics based on what you learn.

3. Use the Resources: Take advantage of the templates, checklists, and additional resources provided in the appendix. These tools are designed to make your marketing efforts more efficient and effective.

4. Stay Updated: Facebook is constantly evolving, and so should your marketing strategies. Use this guide as a living document, regularly updating your knowledge and tactics to stay ahead of the curve.

Kick start on this journey with an open mind and a commitment to learning and experimenting. With "The Facebook Marketing Secrets Guide" in your hands, you're equipped with the knowledge and tools to transform your Facebook marketing efforts and achieve unprecedented growth. Let's dive in and unlock the full potential of Facebook marketing for your business!

Why Facebook? Understanding Its Power and Reach

Facebook isn't just a social network; it's a powerful marketing platform that can transform the way you connect with customers and grow your business.

With over 2.8 billion monthly active users, Facebook offers an unparalleled opportunity to reach a vast and diverse audience.

Here's a closer look at why Facebook should be at the core of your marketing strategy:

1. Global Reach

Facebook's user base spans every corner of the globe, allowing businesses to connect with potential customers worldwide. Whether your target audience is local, national, or international, Facebook's extensive reach ensures that your message can travel far and wide.

2. Advanced Targeting Capabilities

One of Facebook's standout features is its sophisticated targeting options. You can define your audience based on demographics, interests, behaviors, and even specific life events. This level of precision ensures that your ads are seen by the people most likely to be interested in your products or services, maximizing your return on investment.

3. Variety of Engagement Tools

Facebook provides numerous ways to engage with your audience. From posts and stories to live videos and interactive polls, you can create dynamic content that captures attention and fosters interaction. These engagement tools help build a loyal community around your brand, encouraging ongoing conversations and connections.

4. Robust Analytics and Insights

Facebook's analytics tools give you access to detailed insights about your audience and how they interact with your content. You can track metrics such as reach, engagement, and conversion rates, allowing you to measure the effectiveness of your campaigns and make data-driven decisions to improve performance.

5. Cost-Effective Advertising

Facebook ads are known for being cost-effective, offering a high return on investment. You can set your budget and bid amount, ensuring that your advertising spend is controlled and efficient. With options like pay-per-click and pay-per-impression, you can choose the model that best suits your campaign goals and budget.

6. Integration with Other Platforms

Facebook seamlessly integrates with other marketing tools and platforms, enhancing your overall digital marketing strategy. You can connect your Facebook campaigns with Instagram, Messenger, and WhatsApp, creating a cohesive and multi-channel approach to reach your audience.

7. Continuous Innovation

Facebook is constantly evolving, introducing new features and tools to help businesses succeed. Staying updated with these innovations allows you to leverage the latest trends and technologies, keeping your marketing strategies fresh and competitive.

Facebook's power and reach make it an indispensable tool for any marketer looking to make a significant impact. By utilizing Facebook's advanced targeting capabilities, engagement tools, and robust analytics, you can create highly effective marketing campaigns that resonate with your audience and drive meaningful results. Embrace the opportunities Facebook offers and watch your business thrive in the digital age.

How to Use This Guide for Maximum Results

"The Facebook Marketing Secrets Guide" is designed to be your comprehensive companion on the journey to mastering Facebook marketing. Whether you're starting from scratch or looking to enhance your existing efforts, this guide provides step-by-step instructions, expert tips, and real-life examples to ensure your success.

How to make the most of this guide:

1. Follow the Chapters Sequentially

Each chapter is structured to build on the previous one, ensuring a logical progression that covers all aspects of Facebook marketing. Starting with foundational concepts and moving towards advanced strategies, following the chapters in order will help you develop a strong, cohesive understanding of the platform.

2. Apply What You Learn

Reading about strategies and techniques is just the beginning. To truly benefit from this guide, actively apply the knowledge to your own Facebook marketing efforts. Experiment with different approaches, monitor your results, and refine your tactics based on what works best for your audience and goals.

3. Utilize the Provided Resources

The appendix includes valuable resources such as templates, checklists, and additional reading materials. These tools are designed to make your marketing efforts more efficient and effective. Make sure to use them to streamline your planning, execution, and analysis processes.

4. Engage with Real-Life Examples

Throughout the guide, you'll find case studies and success stories that illustrate the concepts and strategies discussed. Pay close attention to these examples, as they provide practical insights and inspiration that you can adapt to your own campaigns.

5. Stay Updated with Facebook's Features

Facebook is a dynamic platform that frequently updates its features and algorithms. To stay ahead of the curve, make a habit of regularly checking for new updates and features. Adapt your strategies to incorporate these changes and ensure your marketing efforts remain effective.

6. Leverage the Community

Join Facebook marketing groups and forums to connect with other marketers and business owners. Sharing experiences, asking questions, and learning from others can provide additional insights and support as you implement the strategies from this guide.

7. Measure and Analyze Your Results

Regularly monitor your campaigns using Facebook's analytics tools. Track key metrics such as reach, engagement, and conversion rates to evaluate the performance of your marketing efforts. Use this data to make informed decisions and continuously improve your strategies.

8. Be Patient and Persistent

Success in Facebook marketing doesn't happen overnight. It requires consistent effort, experimentation, and adaptation. Stay patient, keep learning, and don't be afraid to tweak your strategies based on the insights you gather along the way.

9. Seek Continuous Learning

The world of digital marketing is ever-evolving. To keep your skills sharp and strategies effective, commit to ongoing learning. Read industry blogs, attend webinars, and participate in professional development opportunities related to social media marketing.

Kick start on this journey with an open mind and a commitment to learning and experimenting. With "The Facebook Marketing Secrets Guide" in your hands, you're equipped with the knowledge and tools to transform your Facebook marketing efforts and achieve unprecedented growth. Dive in, apply the strategies, and watch your business thrive in the digital age!

Chapter 1: Building Your Facebook Marketing Foundation

Creating a strong foundation is essential for any successful Facebook marketing strategy. In this chapter, we'll explore the fundamental steps to establish your presence on Facebook and lay the groundwork for effective marketing campaigns.

1. Setting Up Your Business Page: A Step-by-Step Guide

Your Facebook Business Page serves as the cornerstone of your online presence. Follow these steps to create a compelling and professional page:

- **Choose the Right Category:** Select the appropriate category that best represents your business, whether it's a local business, brand, organization, or public figure.
- **Complete Your Profile:** Fill out all relevant information about your business, including your

address, contact details, website URL, and a brief description.
- **Design Your Profile and Cover Photos:** Use high-quality images that reflect your brand identity and showcase what your business is all about.
- **Customize Your Page Tabs:** Arrange your page tabs to highlight important sections such as About, Services, Events, and Reviews.

2. Defining Your Marketing Goals

Before diving into Facebook marketing, it's crucial to clarify your objectives. Ask yourself:

- **What do you aim to achieve with your Facebook presence?** Whether it's increasing brand awareness, driving website traffic, generating leads, or boosting sales, defining clear goals will guide your strategy.
- **Who is your target audience?** Understanding your audience's demographics, interests, and behaviors will help you tailor your content and messaging to resonate with them effectively.

3. Identifying and Understanding Your Target Audience

Knowing your audience is key to creating relevant and engaging content that drives results.

How to identify and understand your target audience:

- **Conduct Market Research:** Use Facebook Insights, surveys, and customer feedback to gain insights into your audience's preferences, challenges, and pain points.
- **Create Buyer Personas:** Develop detailed profiles of your ideal customers, including demographic information, interests, motivations, and purchasing behaviors.
- **Segment Your Audience:** Divide your audience into distinct segments based on demographics, interests, or buying stage. This allows you to deliver personalized content tailored to each group's needs and preferences.

4. Crafting a Compelling Brand Story

Your brand story is what sets you apart from the competition and resonates with your audience on a deeper level.

Here's how to craft a compelling narrative:

- **Define Your Brand Identity:** Clearly articulate your brand's mission, values, and unique selling proposition (USP).
- **Tell Your Story Authentically:** Share the journey behind your brand, including its origins, challenges, and triumphs. Be genuine and transparent in your storytelling.
- **Showcase Your Brand Personality:** Use your brand voice and tone consistently across all communications to build familiarity and trust with your audience.

By laying a solid foundation for your Facebook marketing efforts, you set yourself up for long-term success. In the following chapters, we'll delve deeper into content creation, advertising strategies, and performance tracking to help you achieve your marketing goals effectively.

Setting Up Your Business Page: A Step-by-Step Guide

Setting up your business page on Facebook is the first step towards establishing a strong online presence and connecting with your audience. Follow this step-by-step guide to create a compelling and professional page:

Step 1: Create Your Page

1. Go to Facebook: Log in to your personal Facebook account or create one if you don't have one already.
2. Navigate to Pages: Click on the "Pages" tab on the left-hand side of your Facebook homepage.
3. Create a New Page: Click on the "+ Create" button and select "Page" from the dropdown menu.
4. Choose Your Page Type: Select the type of page that best represents your business, such as

"Business or Brand" or "Community or Public Figure."

5. Enter Your Page Name: Enter the name of your business or brand. Make sure it accurately reflects your business identity and is easy to remember.

6. Add Category and Description: Choose a category that best describes your business and write a brief description that highlights what your page is about.

Step 2: Customize Your Page

1. Upload Profile Picture: Choose a high-quality profile picture that represents your brand, such as your logo or a professional photo of your team.

2. Add a Cover Photo: Select an eye-catching cover photo that showcases your brand personality or features your products/services.

3. Complete About Section: Fill out all relevant information in the "About" section, including your business address, phone number, website URL, and a brief description.

4. Customize Page Tabs: Rearrange your page tabs to prioritize the most important sections, such as "About," "Services," "Events," and "Reviews."

5. Create a Username: Choose a username (also known as a vanity URL) for your page to make it easier for people to find and remember your page.

Step 3: Add Additional Details

1. Provide Contact Information: Make it easy for customers to reach you by adding your contact details, including email address, phone number, and business hours.

2. Add Business Details: Fill in additional details about your business, such as your story, mission, and products/services offered.

3. Set Up Action Buttons: Add action buttons to your page, such as "Call Now," "Book Now," or "Shop Now," to encourage visitors to take specific actions.

Step 4: Review and Publish Your Page

1. Review Your Page: Double-check all the information you've entered to ensure accuracy and completeness.

2. Preview Your Page: Use the "Preview" feature to see how your page will appear to visitors.

3. Publish Your Page: Once you're satisfied with your page setup, click the "Publish" button to make your page live.

Congratulations! You've successfully set up your business page on Facebook. Now it's time to start sharing engaging content, interacting with your audience, and growing your online community.

Defining Your Marketing Goals

Defining clear and actionable marketing goals is essential for guiding your Facebook marketing strategy and measuring your success.

How to define your marketing goals effectively:

1. Identify Your Overall Business Objectives

Begin by understanding your broader business objectives. What are you aiming to achieve as a company? Your marketing goals should align with these objectives and contribute to the overall success of your business. Common business objectives may include increasing revenue, expanding market share, building brand awareness, or launching a new product/service.

2. Make Your Goals Specific, Measurable, Achievable, Relevant, and Time-Bound (SMART)

When setting marketing goals, follow the SMART framework:

- **Specific:** Clearly define what you want to accomplish. Avoid vague objectives like "increase sales" and instead specify a target, such as "increase online sales by 20%."
- **Measurable:** Identify key performance indicators (KPIs) that you can use to track your progress. This could include metrics like website traffic, conversion

rates, lead generation, or social media engagement.

- **Achievable:** Set goals that are realistic and attainable based on your resources, capabilities, and market conditions. Stretch yourself, but avoid setting unattainable targets that may demotivate your team.

- **Relevant:** Ensure that your goals are relevant to your business objectives and directly contribute to your overall success. Focus on outcomes that have a meaningful impact on your bottom line.

- **Time-Bound:** Establish a timeframe or deadline for achieving your goals. This creates a sense of urgency and helps keep your team focused and accountable. For example, "increase email subscribers by 10% within six months."

3. Consider Different Types of Marketing Goals

Depending on your business objectives and stage of growth, your marketing goals may vary.

Common types of marketing goals on Facebook include:

- **Increasing Brand Awareness:** Boosting brand visibility and recognition among your target audience.

- **Generating Leads:** Capturing contact information from potential customers interested in your products or services.

- **Driving Website Traffic:** Directing users to visit your website to learn more about your offerings.

- **Increasing Engagement:** Encouraging likes, comments, shares, and other interactions with your content.

- **Boosting Sales:** Converting leads into paying customers and driving revenue growth.

- **Improving Customer Loyalty:** Fostering long-term relationships with existing customers and encouraging repeat purchases.

4. Prioritize and Focus on a Few Key Goals

While it's tempting to pursue multiple objectives simultaneously, it's often more effective to prioritize a few key goals at a time. Focus on the goals that will have the greatest impact on your business and allocate your resources accordingly. Once you've achieved success with one set of goals, you can then expand your efforts to tackle additional objectives.

By defining clear, specific, and measurable marketing goals, you provide direction and purpose to your Facebook marketing efforts. Regularly review and adjust your goals as needed based on changing market conditions, business priorities, and performance metrics. With a well-defined roadmap in place, you'll be better equipped to achieve meaningful results and drive sustainable growth for your business.

Identifying and Understanding Your Target Audience

Identifying and understanding your target audience is crucial for creating relevant and engaging Facebook marketing campaigns that resonate with your potential customers.

Step-by-step guide to help you define and understand your target audience effectively:

1. Conduct Market Research

Start by gathering information about your target market to gain insights into their demographics, preferences, behaviors, and needs.

Some methods to conduct market research:

- Surveys and Questionnaires: Create surveys or questionnaires to collect data directly from your audience. Ask questions about their age, gender, location, interests, purchasing habits, and pain points.
- Social Media Listening: Monitor social media platforms, forums, and online communities related to your industry to observe conversations, trends, and sentiment among your target audience.
- Competitor Analysis: Study your competitors' social media presence and audience demographics to identify common characteristics and preferences among your shared target audience.

- **Customer Feedback:** Collect feedback from your existing customers through reviews, testimonials, and direct communication to understand their experiences, preferences, and needs.

2. Create Buyer Personas

Based on the insights gathered from your market research, develop detailed buyer personas that represent your ideal customers. A buyer persona is a semi-fictional representation of your target audience, including demographic information, interests, goals, challenges, and purchasing behaviors. Consider factors such as:

- **Demographics:** Age, gender, location, education, occupation, income level, marital status, and family size.
- **Psychographics:** Interests, hobbies, lifestyle, values, beliefs, attitudes, personality traits, and online behaviors.
- **Goals and Challenges:** Identify the goals and objectives your audience is trying to achieve and

the challenges or pain points they encounter along the way.

- **Buying Behavior:** Understand how your audience researches products/services, makes purchasing decisions, and interacts with brands.

3. Segment Your Audience

Once you've developed your buyer personas, segment your audience into distinct groups based on shared characteristics, interests, or behaviors. By segmenting your audience, you can tailor your marketing messages, content, and offers to resonate with each group's specific needs and preferences. Common segmentation criteria include:

- **Demographic Segmentation:** Dividing your audience based on demographic factors such as age, gender, income, and education.
- **Psychographic Segmentation:** Grouping your audience based on shared interests, values, lifestyles, attitudes, and personality traits.

- **Behavioral Segmentation:** Segmenting your audience based on their past behaviors, interactions, purchase history, and engagement with your brand.

4. Validate and Refine Your Audience Insights

Regularly validate and refine your audience insights through ongoing research, testing, and analysis. Monitor the performance of your Facebook marketing campaigns, track key metrics, and solicit feedback from your audience to ensure that your targeting remains accurate and effective. Adjust your buyer personas and segmentation criteria as needed based on evolving market trends, customer feedback, and business objectives.

By identifying and understanding your target audience on Facebook, you can create personalized and relevant marketing campaigns that connect with your potential customers, drive engagement, and ultimately, achieve your business goals. Continuously refine your audience insights to stay aligned with your audience's preferences and behaviors, and adapt your Facebook marketing strategies accordingly for long-term success.

Crafting a Compelling Brand Story

Crafting a compelling brand story is essential for establishing an emotional connection with your audience, differentiating your brand, and creating a lasting impression.

How to create a brand story that captivates and resonates with your target audience:

1. Define Your Brand Identity

Before crafting your brand story, it's essential to clearly define your brand identity, including your mission, values, personality, and unique selling proposition (USP). Ask yourself:

- What is the purpose of your brand? What problem do you solve or what aspiration do you fulfill for your customers?

- What values and beliefs does your brand stand for? What sets you apart from competitors?
- What personality traits best represent your brand? Is your brand playful, authoritative, innovative, or empathetic?
- What makes your brand unique? What benefits or value do you offer to your customers that competitors do not?

2. Understand Your Audience

To create a brand story that resonates with your audience, you must understand their needs, desires, aspirations, and pain points. Conduct market research, develop buyer personas, and gather insights into your audience's demographics, interests, motivations, and challenges. Tailor your brand story to address their specific needs and connect with their emotions.

3. Craft Your Narrative

Your brand story should be authentic, compelling, and memorable. Consider the following elements when crafting your narrative:

- **Introduction:** Start by introducing your brand and setting the stage for your story. Explain who you are, what you do, and why you do it.
- **Conflict or Challenge:** Every compelling story has a conflict or challenge that needs to be overcome. Highlight the challenges your audience faces and how your brand can help them overcome these obstacles.
- **Resolution or Transformation:** Show how your brand provides solutions to your audience's problems or helps them achieve their goals. Share success stories, testimonials, or case studies that illustrate the positive impact your brand has had on customers' lives.
- **Call to Action:** Inspire your audience to take action by inviting them to engage with your brand, whether it's making a purchase, signing up for your newsletter, or following you on social media.

4. Use Emotion and Imagery

Emotion is a powerful tool for storytelling. Use emotive language, vivid imagery, and storytelling techniques to evoke emotions and create a memorable brand experience. Show, don't just tell, your brand story through compelling visuals, videos, and multimedia content that resonate with your audience on an emotional level.

5. Be Authentic and Transparent

Authenticity and transparency are essential elements of a compelling brand story. Be honest about your brand's values, successes, and challenges. Share behind-the-scenes glimpses of your brand's journey, team members, and processes to humanize your brand and build trust with your audience.

6. Consistency Across Channels

Ensure consistency in your brand story across all touchpoints and channels, including your website, social media, advertising, packaging, and customer service. Maintain a cohesive brand voice, tone, and visual identity to reinforce your brand story and strengthen brand recognition.

Crafting a compelling brand story takes time, creativity, and strategic thinking. By aligning your story with your brand identity, understanding your audience's needs, and leveraging emotion and authenticity, you can create a brand narrative that captivates your audience, builds brand loyalty, and drives meaningful connections.

Chapter 2: Content Creation and Engagement Strategies

Creating engaging content is the cornerstone of a successful Facebook marketing strategy. Your content should resonate with your audience, reflect your brand's identity, and encourage interactions that foster a sense of community. Here's a comprehensive guide on content creation and engagement strategies to help you achieve these goals.

1. Understand Your Audience's Preferences

Before creating content, it's crucial to understand what your audience likes and engages with. Analyze your past posts and those of competitors to identify patterns in high-performing content. Use Facebook Insights to gather data on:

- **Post Types:** Determine whether your audience prefers videos, images, text posts, or links.

- **Topics:** Identify the topics that generate the most interest and engagement.
- **Posting Times:** Find out when your audience is most active and likely to engage with your content.

2. Develop a Content Calendar

A content calendar helps you plan and organize your posts in advance, ensuring a consistent and strategic approach. Include:

- **Content Themes:** Decide on overarching themes or topics for each month or week to keep your content focused and relevant.
- **Post Frequency:** Determine how often you will post to maintain a steady presence without overwhelming your audience.
- **Special Events:** Plan content around holidays, industry events, and special promotions.

3. Create High-Quality Visual Content

Visual content is more likely to capture attention and generate engagement. Focus on creating high-quality images and videos that align with your brand identity. Consider the following tips:

- **Professional Photography:** Invest in professional photography to showcase your products or services in the best light.
- **Video Content:** Use videos to tell your brand story, demonstrate products, share customer testimonials, or provide educational content. Facebook Live is an excellent tool for real-time engagement.
- **Graphics and Infographics:** Create visually appealing graphics and infographics to convey information quickly and effectively.

4. Craft Compelling Copy

Your written content should be clear, concise, and engaging. Use compelling headlines, strong calls to action, and a consistent brand voice. Here are some tips:

- **Headlines:** Write attention-grabbing headlines that entice users to click and read more.

- **Brevity:** Keep your posts short and to the point. Use bullet points or lists to make the content easy to digest.

- **Emotional Appeal:** Use storytelling techniques and emotive language to connect with your audience on a deeper level.

5. Encourage User-Generated Content (UGC)

User-generated content is a powerful way to build community and trust. Encourage your audience to share their experiences with your brand. You can:

- **Run Contests and Challenges:** Host contests or challenges that motivate users to create and share content related to your brand.

- **Feature Customer Stories:** Share testimonials, reviews, and user-generated photos or videos on your page.

- **Create Branded Hashtags:** Develop a unique hashtag for your brand and encourage customers to use it when posting about your products or services.

6. Engage with Your Audience

Engagement is a two-way street. Actively interact with your audience to build relationships and foster loyalty. Here's how:

- **Respond to Comments:** Reply to comments on your posts to show that you value your audience's input.
- **Ask Questions:** Post questions to encourage conversations and gather insights from your audience.
- **Host Q&A Sessions:** Use Facebook Live or regular posts to host Q&A sessions where you answer questions from your followers.
- **Create Polls and Surveys:** Engage your audience with interactive polls and surveys to get their opinions and feedback.

7. Analyze and Optimize

Regularly analyze the performance of your content to understand what works and what doesn't. Use Facebook Insights to track key metrics such as reach, engagement, and conversions. Based on your analysis:

- **Identify Top-Performing Content:** Replicate the success of high-performing posts by creating similar content.
- **Adjust Your Strategy:** Make data-driven adjustments to your content strategy to improve performance.
- **Experiment with New Formats:** Continuously test new content formats and ideas to keep your audience engaged.

By implementing these content creation and engagement strategies, you can create a vibrant and active Facebook community that drives brand loyalty and business growth. Remember, the key to success is consistency, creativity, and a deep understanding of your audience's needs and preferences.

Creating Content That Captivates

Creating captivating content on Facebook is essential for capturing your audience's attention and fostering engagement.

Guide to help you develop content that stands out and resonates with your followers:

1. Know Your Audience

Understanding your audience's preferences, interests, and behaviors is crucial for creating relevant content. Use Facebook Insights to gather data on your audience demographics, such as age, gender, location, and interests. Conduct surveys and engage with your audience to gather direct feedback about their content preferences.

2. Use High-Quality Visuals

Visual content is more likely to catch the eye and hold attention. Invest in high-quality images and videos that align with your brand's aesthetic.

Here are some tips:

- **Professional Photography:** Use well-lit, high-resolution photos that showcase your products or services in the best possible light.
- **Engaging Videos:** Create engaging video content, such as tutorials, behind-the-scenes looks, product demos, and customer testimonials. Keep videos concise and to the point.
- **Infographics:** Use infographics to present data or information in a visually appealing and easily digestible format.

3. Craft Compelling Headlines and Captions

Your headlines and captions are the first things your audience will see, so make them count.

Here are some tips for writing compelling copy:

- **Be Clear and Concise:** Ensure your headlines and captions clearly convey the message and grab attention.
- **Use Strong Calls to Action:** Encourage your audience to take action with clear and compelling calls to action (CTAs), such as "Shop Now," "Learn More," or "Join the Conversation."
- **Tell a Story:** Use storytelling techniques to make your captions more engaging and relatable. Share anecdotes, customer stories, or the journey behind your brand.

4. Leverage User-Generated Content

User-generated content (UGC) is a powerful way to build trust and engage your audience. Encourage your followers to create and share content related to your brand. Here's how:

- **Contests and Challenges:** Host contests or challenges that motivate users to create and share content, such as photos, videos, or stories.

- **Feature Customer Stories:** Share testimonials, reviews, and user-generated photos or videos on your page.
- **Create Branded Hashtags:** Develop a unique hashtag for your brand and encourage your audience to use it when posting about your products or services.

5. Utilize Interactive Content

Interactive content encourages participation and engagement. Incorporate these elements into your content strategy:

- **Polls and Surveys:** Use Facebook's poll feature to ask questions and gather feedback from your audience.
- **Quizzes:** Create fun and relevant quizzes that engage your audience and encourage sharing.
- **Live Videos:** Host Facebook Live sessions to interact with your audience in real time, answer questions, and provide valuable insights.

6. Post Consistently and at Optimal Times

Consistency is key to maintaining engagement and building a loyal following. Develop a content calendar to plan and schedule your posts in advance. Use Facebook Insights to determine the optimal times to post based on when your audience is most active.

7. Incorporate Emotional Appeal

Content that evokes emotions tends to perform better. Use storytelling, powerful visuals, and relatable scenarios to connect with your audience on an emotional level. Address their pain points, aspirations, and experiences to make your content more relatable and impactful.

8. Stay Current and Relevant

Keep your content fresh and relevant by staying updated with current events, trends, and industry news. Share timely updates, opinions, and insights that resonate with your audience. Use trending hashtags and participate in popular conversations to increase your content's visibility.

9. Experiment and Innovate

Don't be afraid to experiment with different types of content and formats. Test new ideas, analyze the results, and optimize your strategy based on what works best. Continuous innovation will keep your content exciting and engaging for your audience.

10. Monitor and Analyze Performance

Regularly track and analyze the performance of your content using Facebook Insights. Pay attention to key metrics such as reach, engagement, clicks, and conversions. Use this data to refine your content strategy and improve future posts.

By focusing on these strategies, you can create captivating content that engages your audience, drives interactions, and supports your overall marketing goals. Remember, the key to captivating content is understanding your audience, staying authentic, and continuously evolving your approach based on feedback and performance data.

The Art of Storytelling on Facebook

Storytelling is a powerful tool for capturing attention, building connections, and driving engagement on Facebook. By crafting compelling narratives, you can make your brand more relatable and memorable.

How to master the art of storytelling on Facebook:

1. Understand Your Audience

To tell stories that resonate, you need to understand your audience deeply. Conduct research to gather insights into their demographics, interests, values, and pain points. Use Facebook Insights, surveys, and direct interactions to build a comprehensive picture of who they are and what matters to them.

2. Define Your Brand's Core Story

Your brand's core story is the foundation of your storytelling efforts. It should communicate your mission, values, and unique selling proposition (USP). Here's how to define it:

- **Mission:** What is your brand's purpose? What problem are you solving or what aspiration are you fulfilling?
- **Values:** What principles guide your brand? What do you stand for?
- **USP:** What makes your brand unique? How do you differentiate from competitors?

3. Create a Story Arc

A compelling story has a clear structure with a beginning, middle, and end. Use the classic story arc to shape your narratives:

- **Beginning:** Set the scene and introduce the characters. This is where you grab attention.
- **Middle:** Present the conflict or challenge. This is where you build tension and engage your audience.
- **End:** Show the resolution or transformation. This is where you deliver the message and inspire action.

4. Use Emotion to Connect

Emotions drive engagement. Craft stories that evoke feelings such as joy, surprise, sadness, or inspiration. Use emotive language, vivid imagery, and relatable scenarios to connect with your audience on a deeper level. Remember, people remember how you make them feel more than what you say.

5. Incorporate Visuals

Visual content enhances storytelling by making it more engaging and memorable. Use high-quality photos, videos, and graphics to complement your narrative. Here are some tips:

- **Photos:** Use authentic and expressive images that capture the essence of your story.
- **Videos:** Create dynamic videos that tell your story through motion and sound. Use Facebook Live to share real-time stories and interact with your audience.
- **Graphics:** Use infographics, illustrations, and animations to visualize data and concepts.

6. Highlight Customer Stories

Customer stories and testimonials add credibility and relatability to your brand. Share real-life experiences and success stories from your customers to illustrate the value of your products or services. Encourage customers to share their stories using a branded hashtag.

7. Be Authentic and Transparent

Authenticity builds trust. Be honest about your brand's journey, including successes and challenges. Share behind-the-scenes content to give your audience a glimpse of the people and processes behind your brand. Transparency fosters a sense of connection and loyalty.

8. Create Interactive Stories

Engage your audience by making your stories interactive. Use Facebook's features to encourage participation:

- **Polls and Quizzes:** Ask questions and create quizzes related to your story to engage your audience and gather feedback.
- **Comments and Discussions:** Invite your audience to share their thoughts and experiences in the comments. Respond to their comments to build a two-way dialogue.
- **Live Sessions:** Host Facebook Live sessions to tell stories in real-time and interact with your audience. Answer questions and respond to comments live.

9. Use Data to Refine Your Stories

Regularly analyze the performance of your storytelling efforts using Facebook Insights. Track metrics such as reach, engagement, comments, shares, and conversions. Use this data to understand what resonates with your audience and refine your storytelling strategy accordingly.

10. Consistency is Key

Maintain consistency in your storytelling to reinforce your brand identity. Use a consistent tone, style, and messaging across all your content. Develop a content calendar to plan and schedule your stories in advance, ensuring a steady flow of engaging content.

By mastering the art of storytelling on Facebook, you can create compelling narratives that capture your audience's attention, foster emotional connections, and drive meaningful engagement. Remember, great stories are memorable, relatable, and inspire action. Continuously refine your storytelling approach based on feedback and performance data to keep your audience engaged and connected with your brand.

Utilizing Visuals: Photos, Videos, and Live Streams

Visual content is essential for capturing attention and driving engagement on Facebook. Photos, videos, and live streams are powerful tools that can help you tell your brand's story and connect with your audience.

How to effectively utilize each type of visual content:

1. Photos

High-Quality Images

Invest in high-quality images that are visually appealing and professionally shot. Clear, well-lit, and high-resolution photos can make a significant difference in how your audience perceives your brand.

- Product Photos: Showcase your products from different angles and in various use cases to help potential customers see their value.

- Lifestyle Images: Use lifestyle photos to show your products or services in real-life scenarios. This helps your audience visualize how they can fit into their lives.

- Behind-the-Scenes: Share behind-the-scenes photos to humanize your brand and build a deeper connection with your audience. This can include pictures of your team, workspace, or production process.

Engaging Visuals

- Graphics and Infographics: Use graphics and infographics to present data, statistics, or processes in an easily digestible and visually appealing format.

- **Memes and Quotes:** Create branded memes or quote images to share relatable and engaging content that resonates with your audience.

Tips for Using Photos

- **Consistency:** Maintain a consistent visual style and color scheme that aligns with your brand identity.
- **Captions:** Pair your photos with compelling captions that tell a story or provide context. Use emotive language and clear calls to action.
- **Tags and Hashtags:** Tag relevant people, locations, or products in your photos and use branded hashtags to increase discoverability.

2. Videos

Types of Videos

- **Product Demos:** Create videos that demonstrate how to use your products, highlighting their features and benefits.

- **Tutorials and How-Tos:** Share educational content that provides value to your audience, such as tutorials and how-to videos.
- **Customer Testimonials:** Feature satisfied customers sharing their positive experiences with your brand.
- **Brand Stories:** Use videos to tell your brand's story, share your mission, and showcase your values.

Best Practices for Video Content

- **Short and Sweet:** Keep your videos concise and to the point. Aim for a duration of 1-2 minutes for most videos, as shorter videos tend to have higher engagement rates.
- **Quality Production:** Invest in good lighting, clear audio, and professional editing to ensure your videos are of high quality.
- **Engaging Thumbnails:** Create eye-catching thumbnails that entice users to click and watch your videos.
- **Subtitles and Captions:** Add subtitles or captions to your videos to make them accessible to

a wider audience and to cater to viewers who watch without sound.

3. Live Streams

Benefits of Live Streaming

Live streaming allows you to engage with your audience in real-time, providing an authentic and interactive experience. Use Facebook Live to:

- **Host Q&A Sessions:** Answer questions from your audience live, providing immediate value and fostering a sense of community.
- **Showcase Events:** Stream live events, product launches, or behind-the-scenes tours to give your audience an exclusive look at your brand.
- **Conduct Interviews:** Host interviews with industry experts, influencers, or team members to share insights and build credibility.

Tips for Successful Live Streams

- **Promote in Advance:** Announce your live stream ahead of time to build anticipation and ensure a larger audience.

- **Engage with Viewers:** Interact with your viewers by acknowledging their comments, answering their questions, and responding to their feedback during the live stream.

- **Prepare a Script:** While live streams should feel spontaneous, having a loose script or outline can help you stay on track and cover all important points.

- **Technical Setup:** Ensure you have a stable internet connection, good lighting, and clear audio to provide a seamless viewing experience.

Post-Stream Actions

- **Replay Availability:** Make your live stream replay available on your Facebook page for those who couldn't join live.

- **Engagement:** Continue engaging with viewers by responding to comments and questions even after the live stream has ended.

- **Analyze Performance:** Review the performance metrics of your live stream to understand what worked well and what could be improved for future streams.

By leveraging the power of photos, videos, and live streams, you can create engaging and dynamic content that captures your audience's attention, builds relationships, and drives meaningful interactions on Facebook. Remember, consistency, quality, and authenticity are key to making your visual content stand out and resonate with your audience.

Engaging with Your Audience: Comments, Messages, and Community Building

Engaging with your audience is crucial for building strong relationships, fostering loyalty, and creating a vibrant community around your brand. Facebook offers several ways to interact with your audience, including comments, messages, and community building strategies.

Here's how to effectively engage with your audience on Facebook:

1. Engaging Through Comments

Respond to Comments

- **Prompt Responses:** Respond to comments on your posts promptly. This shows that you value your audience's input and are attentive to their needs.
- **Personalized Replies:** Personalize your replies by addressing commenters by their names and providing thoughtful responses. Avoid generic replies to make your interactions more meaningful.
- **Encourage Conversations:** Ask follow-up questions to keep the conversation going. Engaging discussions can boost your post's visibility and foster a sense of community.

Moderate Comments

- **Positive Reinforcement:** Highlight positive comments and acknowledge them publicly. This can encourage more positive interactions and build a supportive community.

- **Address Negative Feedback:** Handle negative comments professionally and empathetically. Apologize for any issues and offer solutions to resolve problems.

- **Remove Inappropriate Content:** Set clear guidelines for acceptable behavior and remove comments that are offensive, spammy, or violate your community standards.

Engage with Comments on Ads

- **Interactive Ads:** Monitor and respond to comments on your Facebook ads. Engaging with users in the comment section of ads can increase their effectiveness and improve your ad performance.

- **Feedback Loop:** Use comments on ads to gather feedback and insights about your products or services. This can help you refine your offerings and marketing strategies.

2. Engaging Through Messages

Utilize Facebook Messenger

- **Quick Responses:** Respond to messages promptly to provide excellent customer service. Use Facebook's auto-response feature to acknowledge messages instantly when you're not available.
- **Personalized Interactions:** Tailor your responses to each individual to make them feel valued and understood. Use their name and reference previous interactions if applicable.
- **Provide Value:** Offer valuable information, assistance, or exclusive offers through Messenger to enhance the user experience and build loyalty.

3. Community Building

Create and Manage Facebook Groups

- **Exclusive Groups:** Create Facebook Groups for your most loyal customers or specific audience segments. Offer exclusive content, early access to products, and special offers to group members.

- **Active Moderation:** Regularly participate in group discussions, moderate posts, and encourage members to share their experiences and insights.

- **Value-Driven Content:** Share valuable content, such as tips, tutorials, behind-the-scenes looks, and industry news, to keep group members engaged and coming back for more.

Host Events and Webinars

- **Virtual Events:** Host virtual events, such as webinars, Q&A sessions, or live demonstrations, to engage with your audience in real time. Promote these events across your Facebook page and groups.

- **Interactive Elements:** Include interactive elements, such as polls, quizzes, and live chats, to encourage participation and make the events more engaging.

- **Follow-Up Engagement:** After the event, share highlights, answer additional questions, and continue the conversation in your Facebook Group or page.

User-Generated Content (UGC)

- **Encourage UGC:** Invite your audience to share their experiences with your brand by posting photos, videos, and stories. Use branded hashtags to track and showcase user-generated content.
- **Feature UGC:** Highlight user-generated content on your page, in stories, or in marketing campaigns. This not only engages your audience but also builds social proof and credibility.
- **Reward Participation:** Acknowledge and reward users who contribute high-quality content. This could be through shout-outs, giveaways, or exclusive discounts.

Engage with Influencers

- **Collaborations:** Partner with influencers who align with your brand values and have a significant following within your target audience. Collaborative content can expand your reach and engage new audiences.

- **Authenticity:** Ensure that influencer content is authentic and resonates with their audience. Authentic endorsements are more likely to build trust and drive engagement.

- **Engagement Campaigns:** Run influencer-led engagement campaigns, such as contests or challenges, to encourage user participation and increase brand visibility.

By actively engaging with your audience through comments, messages, and community-building efforts, you can create a loyal and vibrant community around your brand. Consistent, meaningful interactions foster trust and loyalty, driving long-term success for your Facebook marketing efforts.

Chapter 3: Mastering Facebook Advertising

Facebook advertising is a powerful tool for reaching your target audience, driving traffic, and increasing conversions. With over 2.8 billion monthly active users, Facebook provides unparalleled opportunities for businesses to connect with potential customers.

How to master Facebook advertising and make the most of this platform:

1. Understanding Facebook Ads Manager

Navigating the Interface

Facebook Ads Manager is the hub for creating, managing, and analyzing your ad campaigns. Familiarize yourself with the key sections:
- **Campaigns:** The overarching structure where you set your objectives.
- **Ad Sets:** Where you define your targeting, budget, and placement options.

- **Ads:** The creative elements that your audience will see.

Setting Up Your Business Manager Account

- **Create an Account:** Sign up for Facebook Business Manager to manage multiple ad accounts, Pages, and team members in one place.
- **Add Assets:** Add your Facebook Page, Instagram account, and any other assets you plan to use.
- **Assign Roles:** Designate roles to team members, such as admin, editor, or advertiser, to streamline workflow and maintain control over your assets.

2. Setting Clear Objectives

Choosing the Right Campaign Objective

Facebook offers various campaign objectives based on your marketing goals:
- **Awareness:** Increase brand awareness or reach as many people as possible.

- **Consideration:** Drive traffic, engagement, app installs, video views, lead generation, or messages.
- **Conversion:** Increase conversions, catalog sales, or store visits.

Aligning Objectives with Business Goals

Ensure your campaign objectives align with your overall business goals. For instance:
- **Brand Awareness:** Use this objective if you're launching a new product or entering a new market.
- **Lead Generation:** Ideal for collecting customer information through forms, especially if you offer services or high-ticket items.
- **Conversions:** Focus on this if you're running an e-commerce store and want to increase sales.

3. Crafting Targeted Ad Sets

Audience Targeting

- **Core Audiences:** Define your audience based on demographics, interests, behaviors, and location.

Use Facebook's detailed targeting options to narrow down your audience.

- **Custom Audiences:** Retarget existing customers or website visitors by uploading your customer list, using Facebook Pixel data, or integrating with your CRM.
- **Lookalike Audiences:** Reach new people who are similar to your existing customers by creating lookalike audiences based on your custom audiences.

Budget and Scheduling

- **Daily vs. Lifetime Budget:** Choose between a daily budget (spend a specific amount each day) or a lifetime budget (spend a specific amount over the entire campaign duration).
- **Ad Scheduling:** Decide whether to run your ads continuously or on a schedule that matches when your target audience is most active.

Placement Options

- **Automatic Placements:** Let Facebook optimize where your ads appear across Facebook, Instagram, Audience Network, and Messenger.
- **Manual Placements:** Choose specific placements to control where your ads are shown. For example, if you find that ads perform better on Instagram Stories, you can allocate more budget there.

4. Creating Compelling Ads

Ad Formats

Facebook offers various ad formats to suit different objectives and creative needs:
- **Image Ads:** Use high-quality images to capture attention. Ideal for straightforward messages and visual appeal.
- **Video Ads:** Engage viewers with compelling video content. Useful for storytelling and demonstrating products.
- **Carousel Ads:** Showcase multiple images or videos within a single ad. Great for highlighting different products or features.

- **Slideshow Ads:** Create lightweight videos from a series of images. Suitable for low-bandwidth regions.
- **Collection Ads:** Combine videos and product images. Perfect for e-commerce to showcase your catalog.
- **Instant Experience:** Create a full-screen, interactive experience on mobile devices.

Ad Copy and Creative

- **Attention-Grabbing Headlines:** Write headlines that immediately capture interest and convey the main message.
- **Compelling Visuals:** Use high-quality images or videos that are relevant to your ad's message and resonate with your target audience.
- **Clear Call to Action:** Include a strong call to action (CTA) that tells users exactly what you want them to do, such as "Shop Now," "Learn More," or "Sign Up."
- **Consistent Branding:** Ensure your ad visuals and copy align with your brand's voice and style to maintain consistency and build recognition.

5. Monitoring and Optimizing Performance

Tracking and Analyzing Metrics

Use Facebook Ads Manager to monitor the performance of your campaigns. Key metrics to track include:

- **Reach and Impressions:** How many people saw your ad and how many times it was shown.
- **Clicks and Click-Through Rate (CTR):** The number of clicks on your ad and the percentage of impressions that resulted in clicks.
- **Conversions:** Actions taken by users, such as purchases, sign-ups, or downloads.
- **Cost Per Action (CPA):** The average cost per desired action, such as a click, lead, or sale.

A/B Testing

- **Split Testing:** Test different versions of your ads to see which performs better. You can test variables such as images, headlines, ad copy, CTAs, and targeting options.

- **Iterative Improvements:** Use the insights from A/B tests to continuously refine and improve your ads. Implement changes based on data to optimize performance.

Retargeting Strategies

- **Dynamic Ads:** Automatically show personalized ads to users based on their interactions with your website or app. This is especially useful for e-commerce sites with large product catalogs.
- **Sequential Retargeting:** Serve a series of ads to guide users through the customer journey. For example, start with a brand awareness ad, followed by a product demo, and finally a promotional offer.

Budget Optimization

- **Automatic Bid Strategies:** Use Facebook's automated bidding options, such as lowest cost or target cost, to maximize your budget's efficiency.
- **Manual Bid Strategies:** Set manual bids if you have specific cost targets or want more control over your ad spend.

By mastering these aspects of Facebook advertising, you can create effective campaigns that drive meaningful results for your business. Continuously monitor performance, experiment with new strategies, and stay up-to-date with Facebook's evolving advertising features to stay ahead of the competition.

Introduction to Facebook Ads

In today's digital landscape, Facebook advertising stands out as one of the most powerful tools for businesses to reach and engage with their target audience. With over 2.8 billion monthly active users, Facebook offers a vast and diverse audience, making it an essential platform for any marketing strategy. Whether you're a small business owner, a marketing professional, or an entrepreneur, understanding how to effectively leverage Facebook ads can significantly enhance your online presence, drive traffic, and increase sales.

Why Facebook Advertising?

Unparalleled Reach and Targeting

Facebook's extensive user base spans across various demographics, locations, and interests. This vast reach allows you to target specific segments of the population with precision. The platform's advanced targeting options enable you to define your audience based on demographics, behaviors, interests, and even life events, ensuring that your ads reach the most relevant users.

Cost-Effective Marketing

Facebook advertising offers flexible budget options, making it accessible for businesses of all sizes. Whether you have a small budget or a large one, you can set daily or lifetime budgets, control your spending, and adjust your bids to maximize your return on investment (ROI). The ability to start with a minimal budget and scale up as you see results makes Facebook ads a cost-effective solution for driving business growth.

Variety of Ad Formats

Facebook provides a wide range of ad formats to suit different marketing objectives and creative needs. From image and video ads to carousel and collection ads, you can choose the format that best showcases your products or services and resonates with your audience. This variety allows for creative flexibility and helps in delivering engaging content that captures attention.

Measurable Results

One of the key advantages of Facebook advertising is the ability to track and measure your campaign's performance in real time. Facebook Ads Manager offers detailed analytics and reporting tools that provide insights into your ad's reach, engagement, conversions, and more. This data-driven approach enables you to make informed decisions, optimize your campaigns, and achieve your marketing goals.

Getting Started with Facebook Ads

Setting Up Your Facebook Business Account

To start advertising on Facebook, you need a Facebook Business Manager account. This centralized platform allows you to manage multiple ad accounts, Pages, and assets securely.

Follow these steps to set up your account:

1. Create a Facebook Business Manager Account: Visit business.facebook.com and sign up for a new account. Enter your business details and complete the setup process.
2. Add Your Facebook Page and Instagram Account: Link your Facebook Page and Instagram account to your Business Manager to manage your ads across both platforms.
3. Set Up Payment Methods: Add your preferred payment methods to ensure smooth billing for your ad campaigns.

Understanding Facebook Ads Manager

Facebook Ads Manager is the main tool for creating, managing, and analyzing your ad campaigns. It consists of three key components:

1. Campaigns: The highest level of your ad structure, where you set your marketing objectives, such as brand awareness, traffic, or conversions.
2. Ad Sets: Within each campaign, you can create multiple ad sets to define your target audience, budget, and placements.
3. Ads: The individual ads within each ad set, where you create the visual and textual content that your audience will see.

Crafting Your First Ad Campaign

Defining Your Marketing Objectives

Before creating your ad, it's crucial to define your marketing objectives. Facebook offers several objectives based on your business goals, including:

- **Awareness:** Increase brand awareness or reach a wide audience.

- **Consideration:** Drive traffic, engagement, app installs, video views, lead generation, or messages.
- **Conversions:** Encourage specific actions such as purchases, sign-ups, or downloads.

Audience Targeting

Effective targeting is the cornerstone of a successful Facebook ad campaign. Utilize Facebook's targeting options to reach your ideal audience:

- **Core Audiences:** Define your audience based on demographics, interests, and behaviors.
- **Custom Audiences:** Retarget existing customers or website visitors by uploading customer lists or using Facebook Pixel data.
- **Lookalike Audiences:** Find new potential customers by creating audiences similar to your existing ones.

Budget and Scheduling

Set your budget and schedule for your ad campaign. Choose between a daily budget (how much you want to spend each day) or a lifetime budget (total amount to spend over the campaign's duration). Schedule your ads to run continuously or during specific times and dates that align with your audience's activity.

Ad Creation

Create compelling ads that capture your audience's attention. Focus on the following elements:

- **Visuals:** Use high-quality images or videos that are relevant to your ad's message and resonate with your target audience.
- **Ad Copy:** Write clear and concise ad copy that highlights your unique selling points and includes a strong call to action (CTA).
- **Landing Page:** Ensure your landing page is optimized and provides a seamless experience for users who click on your ad.

Measuring and Optimizing Your Ads

Tracking Performance

Use Facebook Ads Manager to monitor your ad campaign's performance. Key metrics to track include reach, impressions, clicks, click-through rate (CTR), conversions, and cost per action (CPA). Analyze these metrics to understand how your ads are performing and identify areas for improvement.

A/B Testing

Conduct A/B testing (split testing) to compare different versions of your ads. Test variables such as images, headlines, ad copy, and CTAs to determine which elements drive the best results. Use the insights from A/B testing to refine your ads and optimize your campaigns for better performance.

Continuous Optimization

Facebook advertising is an ongoing process that requires continuous optimization. Regularly review your campaign performance, experiment with new strategies, and adjust your targeting, budget, and creative elements based on data-driven insights. By staying proactive and adaptive, you can maximize your ad spend and achieve your marketing objectives.

Mastering Facebook advertising can transform your business by expanding your reach, driving engagement, and increasing conversions. With a clear understanding of Facebook Ads Manager, well-defined marketing objectives, precise audience targeting, compelling ad creatives, and continuous optimization, you can create effective ad campaigns that deliver tangible results. Embrace the power of Facebook advertising and unlock new growth opportunities for your business.

Crafting Irresistible Ad Copy

Creating compelling ad copy is essential for capturing your audience's attention and driving engagement. Your ad copy should not only inform but also inspire action. Here are the key components and strategies for crafting irresistible ad copy that resonates with your audience and achieves your marketing goals.

1. Understanding Your Audience

Know Your Audience

- **Demographics:** Understand the age, gender, location, and other demographic details of your target audience.
- **Interests and Behaviors:** Identify what interests and behaviors your audience exhibits. This can include hobbies, shopping habits, and online behavior.
- **Pain Points and Needs:** Recognize the problems your audience faces and how your product or service can provide a solution.

Speak Their Language

- **Tone and Style:** Match the tone and style of your copy to your audience's preferences. Whether it's professional, casual, humorous, or inspirational, ensure it resonates with them.

- **Relevant Vocabulary:** Use words and phrases that your audience uses and understands. This helps build a connection and makes your message more relatable.

2. Creating Attention-Grabbing Headlines

The Importance of Headlines

Your headline is the first thing your audience will see, and it needs to capture their attention immediately. A compelling headline can significantly increase the likelihood of your ad being noticed and clicked.

Tips for Effective Headlines

- **Be Clear and Concise:** Your headline should clearly convey what your ad is about. Avoid vague or ambiguous language.
- **Highlight Benefits:** Focus on the benefits of your product or service. What problem does it solve? What value does it offer?

- **Create Urgency:** Use words that create a sense of urgency, such as "Limited Time Offer," "Hurry," or "Don't Miss Out."
- **Ask Questions:** Pose a question that piques curiosity or addresses a common pain point, encouraging users to seek answers by clicking on your ad.

Headline Examples

- "Unlock the Secret to Effortless Weight Loss!"
- "Limited Time Offer: 50% Off All Summer Dresses!"
- "Struggling with Work-Life Balance? Discover Our Tips!"
- "Is Your Business Ready for the Holiday Rush?"

3. Writing Engaging Ad Copy

Focus on Benefits Over Features

While it's important to mention the features of your product or service, emphasizing the benefits is crucial. Benefits explain how your product or service improves the lives of your customers.

- **Feature:** "Our software includes advanced analytics tools."
- **Benefit:** "Gain deeper insights into your business with our advanced analytics tools."

Keep It Simple and Direct

- **Concise Language:** Avoid unnecessary jargon or complex sentences. Clear and direct language ensures your message is easily understood.
- **Bullet Points:** Use bullet points to highlight key benefits or features, making your copy scannable and easy to read.

Create a Strong Call to Action (CTA)

Your CTA should clearly tell the audience what you want them to do next. Make it compelling and action-oriented.

- **Examples of Strong CTAs:**

- "Shop Now"
- "Sign Up Today"
- "Learn More"
- "Get Started"
- "Download Your Free Guide"

Incorporate Social Proof

Including testimonials, reviews, or endorsements can build trust and credibility. Social proof demonstrates that others have benefited from your product or service.

- **Example:** "Join over 10,000 satisfied customers who have transformed their lives with our fitness program!"

Use Emotional Triggers

Tap into your audience's emotions to create a deeper connection. Emotions such as excitement, fear, happiness, or curiosity can drive action.

- **Example:** "Imagine the joy of opening your dream business. Start your journey with us today!"

4. Optimizing for Mobile

Mobile-Friendly Copy

With a significant portion of users accessing Facebook via mobile devices, ensure your ad copy is mobile-friendly.

- **Short and Sweet:** Keep your copy brief and to the point. Mobile users tend to skim through content.
- **Readable Fonts:** Use fonts that are easy to read on small screens.
- **Engaging Visuals:** Pair your copy with high-quality visuals that enhance your message and capture attention.

Call to Action for Mobile Users

Make sure your CTA buttons are large enough to be easily tapped on mobile devices. Position them prominently so they are not missed.

5. A/B Testing Your Ad Copy

The Importance of A/B Testing

A/B testing allows you to compare different versions of your ad copy to see which one performs better. By testing various elements, you can optimize your ads for maximum effectiveness.

Elements to Test

- **Headlines:** Try different headlines to see which one captures more attention.
- **Ad Copy:** Experiment with different wording, lengths, and styles.
- **CTAs:** Test various calls to action to determine which one drives more conversions.
- **Visuals:** Combine different images or videos with your ad copy to see which combination works best.

Analyzing Results

Use Facebook Ads Manager to track the performance of your A/B tests. Look at metrics such as click-through rate (CTR), conversion rate, and cost per click (CPC) to determine the most effective copy.

6. Continuous Improvement

Monitor and Adjust

Regularly monitor the performance of your ads and be ready to make adjustments. The digital landscape is dynamic, and what works today might not work tomorrow.

Stay Updated

Keep up with the latest trends and best practices in Facebook advertising. Attend webinars, read industry blogs, and participate in forums to stay informed.

Learn from Competitors

Analyze the ad strategies of your competitors. Identify what works well for them and consider how you can implement similar tactics in your campaigns.

By crafting irresistible ad copy, you can effectively capture the attention of your audience, communicate your value proposition, and drive meaningful actions. Focus on understanding your audience, creating compelling headlines, writing engaging copy, optimizing for mobile, and continuously testing and improving your ads. With these strategies, you'll be well on your way to mastering the art of Facebook advertising.

Choosing the Right Ad Format for Your Goals

Facebook offers a variety of ad formats, each tailored to different marketing objectives and audience engagement strategies. Selecting the right ad format for your goals is crucial for maximizing the effectiveness of your campaigns. Here's a comprehensive guide to help you choose the best ad format for your specific marketing objectives.

1. Awareness Objectives

Objective: Increase brand awareness or reach a broad audience.

Recommended Ad Formats:

- Image Ads: Simple yet effective, image ads use high-quality visuals to capture attention and convey a clear message. Ideal for showcasing products, announcing events, or highlighting brand values.

- Video Ads: Engaging and dynamic, video ads can tell a story, demonstrate products, or share customer testimonials. Videos can be short and impactful, making them perfect for brand awareness campaigns.

Best Practices:

- Use eye-catching visuals and concise messaging.
- Ensure your brand logo and key message are visible within the first few seconds of the video.

2. Consideration Objectives

Objective: Drive traffic, engagement, app installs, video views, lead generation, or messages.

Recommended Ad Formats:

- **Carousel Ads:** Showcase multiple images or videos within a single ad. Great for highlighting different products, features, or benefits. Each card in the carousel can have its own link, driving traffic to various pages.

- **Slideshow Ads:** Create lightweight video ads from a series of images. These are suitable for reaching audiences in regions with slower internet connections.

- **Collection Ads:** Combine videos and product images to create a visually rich and interactive shopping experience. When users tap on the ad, they can browse through a collection of products within Facebook.

- Lead Ads: Designed to collect user information directly on Facebook, lead ads are perfect for gathering email sign-ups, newsletter subscriptions, or demo requests without users leaving the platform.

- Instant Experience (Canvas) Ads: A full-screen, immersive ad format for mobile devices. Instant Experience ads are ideal for showcasing a brand story, catalog, or product details interactively.

Best Practices:
- Use engaging visuals and clear CTAs for each ad format.
- Keep the user experience seamless and intuitive.
- Personalize content to increase relevance and engagement.

3. Conversion Objectives

Objective: Encourage specific actions such as purchases, sign-ups, or downloads.

Recommended Ad Formats:

- **Single Image Ads:** Direct and focused, these ads drive users to take action with a clear and compelling CTA. Perfect for promoting limited-time offers or specific products.

- **Dynamic Ads:** Automatically show the right products to users who have expressed interest on your website or app. Ideal for e-commerce businesses, dynamic ads use Facebook Pixel data to retarget users with personalized product recommendations.

- **Collection Ads:** As with consideration objectives, collection ads also work well for driving conversions by providing a seamless shopping experience within the Facebook app.

- **Messenger Ads:** Encourage direct communication with potential customers by placing ads in the Messenger app. Great for personalized customer service, order confirmations, and nurturing leads.

Best Practices:
- Highlight the unique selling points and benefits of your products or services.
- Use strong CTAs that prompt immediate action, such as "Buy Now" or "Sign Up Today."
- Ensure landing pages are optimized for conversions and provide a consistent experience.

4. App Install Objectives

Objective: Increase app installations and engagement.

Recommended Ad Formats:

- **App Install Ads:** Specifically designed to promote app installations, these ads can appear in the news feed or in the Audience Network. They include a direct link to the app store, making it easy for users to download your app.

- **Video Ads:** Showcase your app's features and benefits through engaging video content. Demonstrating how your app works and its unique value proposition can drive more installations.

Best Practices:
- Use clear and enticing visuals or videos that highlight your app's key features.
- Include a compelling CTA, such as "Install Now" or "Download Today."
- Target users based on their interests and behaviors to increase the likelihood of installs.

5. Engagement Objectives

Objective: Increase interactions such as likes, shares, comments, and overall engagement with your content.

Recommended Ad Formats:

- **Post Engagement Ads:** Boost existing posts to increase visibility and engagement. This format is excellent for promoting organic content, such as blog posts, videos, or user-generated content.

- Event Response Ads: Promote your events to get more responses and attendance. These ads are designed to increase event awareness and participation.

- Page Like Ads: Specifically aimed at increasing your page's follower count. These ads encourage users to like your page, helping to build a larger and more engaged audience.

Best Practices:
- Create content that encourages interaction, such as questions, polls, or user-generated content.
- Use high-quality visuals and engaging copy to capture attention and provoke responses.
- Monitor engagement metrics and respond to comments to foster community building.

Choosing the right ad format for your goals on Facebook is crucial for the success of your campaigns. By aligning your ad formats with your marketing objectives, you can create more effective and engaging ads that drive meaningful results. Whether your goal is to increase brand awareness, drive traffic, generate leads, or boost conversions, Facebook offers a versatile range of ad formats to help you achieve your targets.

Advanced Targeting Techniques: Custom Audiences and Lookalikes

To maximize the impact of your Facebook advertising campaigns, leveraging advanced targeting techniques is crucial. Two of the most powerful tools at your disposal are Custom Audiences and Lookalike Audiences. These targeting options allow you to reach highly specific groups of users who are more likely to engage with your ads and convert into customers. This section will guide you through the process of creating and using Custom Audiences and Lookalike Audiences effectively.

1. Custom Audiences

What Are Custom Audiences?

Custom Audiences allow you to target your ads to people who have already interacted with your business. This could include customers who have visited your website, engaged with your app, or are part of your email list. By targeting users who are already familiar with your brand, you can increase the relevance and effectiveness of your ads.

Creating Custom Audiences

There are several methods to create Custom Audiences:

- **Customer List:** Upload a list of customer information such as email addresses, phone numbers, or Facebook user IDs. Facebook matches this data with user profiles to create your Custom Audience.

- **Website Traffic:** Use Facebook Pixel to track visitors to your website. You can create audiences

107

based on specific pages they visited, the time they spent on your site, or the actions they took (e.g., adding items to their cart).

- App Activity: Track user interactions within your mobile app. You can create audiences based on in-app actions, such as completed purchases or achieved milestones.

- Engagement: Create audiences from people who have engaged with your content on Facebook or Instagram. This includes video views, lead form completions, page likes, and event responses.

Setting Up a Custom Audience

1. Go to Ads Manager: Navigate to the Audiences section in Facebook Ads Manager.
2. Create Audience: Click on the "Create Audience" button and select "Custom Audience."
3. Choose Your Source: Select the source of your Custom Audience (e.g., customer list, website traffic).

4. Upload Data or Define Criteria: If using a customer list, upload your data file. If using website traffic or app activity, define the criteria for your audience.

5. Name Your Audience: Give your Custom Audience a descriptive name to easily identify it later.

Benefits of Custom Audiences

- **Re-engage Existing Customers:** Target previous customers with new offers or remind them of items left in their cart.
- **Increase Relevance:** Ads shown to people who are already familiar with your brand are more likely to perform well.
- **Personalize Messaging:** Tailor your ad copy and creatives to resonate with users based on their previous interactions with your business.

2. Lookalike Audiences

What Are Lookalike Audiences?

Lookalike Audiences allow you to reach new people who are similar to your existing customers or audience members. Facebook analyzes the characteristics of your source audience and finds users with similar traits, behaviors, and interests.

Creating Lookalike Audiences

1. Select a Source Audience: Your source audience can be a Custom Audience, your Facebook Page fans, or any other audience segment you've created.

2. Define the Audience Size: Choose the size of your Lookalike Audience. A smaller percentage (e.g., 1%) will be more similar to your source audience, while a larger percentage (e.g., 10%) will reach a broader audience but may be less similar.

3. Specify the Location: Select the country or region where you want to find your Lookalike Audience.

4. Create the Audience: Facebook will generate a Lookalike Audience based on the parameters you set.

Setting Up a Lookalike Audience

1. Go to Ads Manager: Navigate to the Audiences section in Facebook Ads Manager.

2. Create Audience: Click on the "Create Audience" button and select "Lookalike Audience."

3. Choose Your Source: Select your source audience. This could be a Custom Audience, page fans, or any other audience segment.

4. Select Location and Size: Specify the location and size of your Lookalike Audience.

5. Name Your Audience: Give your Lookalike Audience a descriptive name for easy identification.

Benefits of Lookalike Audiences

- **Expand Reach:** Reach new users who are likely to be interested in your business because they share characteristics with your existing customers.

- **Optimize Ad Spend:** By targeting users similar to your best customers, you can achieve higher conversion rates and a better return on investment (ROI).

- **Simplify Targeting:** Lookalike Audiences simplify the targeting process by automatically identifying potential customers who are similar to your known audience.

3. Combining Custom Audiences and Lookalike Audiences

Strategies for Effective Use

- **Sequential Advertising:** Use Custom Audiences to retarget users who have interacted with your brand, then expand your reach with Lookalike Audiences to find new potential customers.
- **Exclude Overlapping Audiences:** When creating Lookalike Audiences, exclude your existing customers or specific Custom Audiences to avoid showing ads to the same people repeatedly.
- **A/B Testing:** Test different ad creatives and messages on Custom Audiences and Lookalike Audiences to see which performs better and refine your approach accordingly.

Example Campaigns

- **Retargeting Campaign:** Create a Custom Audience of users who visited your website but didn't make a purchase. Show them ads with a special discount to encourage them to complete their purchase.

- **Prospecting Campaign:** Use a Lookalike Audience based on your top customers to find new potential buyers. Promote your best-selling products or latest offers to attract these new users.

Utilizing Custom Audiences and Lookalike Audiences can significantly enhance your Facebook advertising efforts. By targeting users who are already familiar with your brand and finding new potential customers who share similar characteristics, you can create more effective and efficient ad campaigns. Implement these advanced targeting techniques to boost your engagement, conversions, and overall ROI.

A/B Testing and Optimizing Your Ads

To maximize the effectiveness of your Facebook ad campaigns, continuous testing and optimization are essential. A/B testing, also known as split testing, allows you to compare different versions of your ads to determine which performs better. This section will guide you through the process of setting up A/B tests and optimizing your ads based on the results.

1. The Importance of A/B Testing

A/B testing helps you understand what resonates with your audience and allows you to make data-driven decisions. By testing different elements of your ads, you can:

- **Increase Engagement:** Identify the ad variations that capture attention and drive interaction.
- **Improve Conversion Rates:** Find the most effective combination of visuals, copy, and CTAs to convert viewers into customers.

- **Optimize Ad Spend:** Allocate your budget to the best-performing ads, maximizing your return on investment (ROI).

2. Setting Up an A/B Test

Step 1: Define Your Objective

Start by clearly defining what you want to achieve with your A/B test. Common objectives include:

- Increasing click-through rates (CTR)
- Boosting conversions
- Reducing cost per acquisition (CPA)
- Enhancing engagement (likes, shares, comments)

Step 2: Choose Your Variables

Identify the elements of your ad that you want to test. Common variables include:

- **Headlines:** Test different headlines to see which one grabs attention.

- **Ad Copy:** Experiment with different messages and tones.
- **Images/Videos:** Compare different visuals to see which is more engaging.
- **Call-to-Actions (CTAs):** Test different CTAs to find the most compelling one.
- **Targeting Options:** Experiment with different audience segments to identify the most responsive group.

Step 3: Create Your Ad Variations

For each variable you want to test, create different versions. For example, if you're testing headlines, you might create two ads with identical images and copy but different headlines.

Step 4: Set Up the Test in Ads Manager

1. Go to Ads Manager: Navigate to the Experiments section in Facebook Ads Manager.
2. Create A/B Test: Click on "Create A/B Test" and select the campaign or ad set you want to test.

3. Select Variable: Choose the variable you want to test (e.g., creative, audience, placement).

4. Create Variations: Input your different ad variations.

5. Set Budget and Schedule: Allocate your budget and set the duration of the test.

Step 5: Run the Test

Launch your A/B test and allow it to run for a sufficient period to gather meaningful data. Facebook recommends running tests for at least 7 days to ensure you have enough data for accurate results.

3. Analyzing A/B Test Results

Once your A/B test has concluded, it's time to analyze the results. Look at key metrics such as:

- **CTR (Click-Through Rate):** Measures the percentage of people who clicked on your ad.

- **Conversion Rate:** Measures the percentage of users who completed a desired action (e.g., purchase, sign-up).
- **CPA (Cost Per Acquisition):** Measures the cost of acquiring a new customer or lead.
- **Engagement:** Looks at likes, shares, comments, and other forms of interaction.

Facebook Ads Manager provides detailed reports on your test results. Compare the performance of each variation to identify the winner.

4. Optimizing Your Ads Based on Results

Implement the Winning Variation

Once you've identified the best-performing ad variation, implement it in your campaign. Use the insights gained to inform future ad creation and targeting strategies.

Iterate and Test Further

A/B testing is an ongoing process. Continually test new variations to keep improving your ad performance. Here are some additional areas to test:

- **Ad Frequency:** Test different frequencies to find the optimal balance between exposure and ad fatigue.
- **Ad Placements:** Experiment with different ad placements (e.g., news feed, stories, right column) to see where your ads perform best.
- **Audience Segmentation:** Test different audience segments based on demographics, interests, and behaviors.

Refine Your Targeting

Use the insights from your A/B tests to refine your targeting. For example, if a particular audience segment responds well to a certain type of ad, consider creating more tailored ads for that segment.

5. Best Practices for A/B Testing

Test One Variable at a Time

To accurately determine what's driving performance changes, test only one variable at a time. Testing multiple variables simultaneously can make it difficult to identify which change led to the results.

Use a Large Enough Sample Size

Ensure your test reaches a sufficient number of users to generate statistically significant results. Small sample sizes can lead to unreliable conclusions.

Allow Tests to Run Long Enough

Give your tests enough time to gather meaningful data. Short tests may not capture the full picture of user behavior.

Maintain Consistency

Ensure that all other elements of your campaign remain constant during the test period. Changes in budget, targeting, or external factors can skew your results.

Document Your Findings

Keep a record of your A/B test results and insights. This documentation can help you track what works over time and apply successful strategies to future campaigns.

A/B testing and optimizing your ads is a continuous process that can significantly improve your Facebook advertising performance. By systematically testing different elements of your ads and making data-driven decisions, you can enhance engagement, increase conversions, and optimize your ad spend. Implement these strategies to create more effective and impactful Facebook ad campaigns.

Chapter 4: Analytics and Performance Tracking

Understanding how your Facebook ads perform is crucial to the success of your marketing campaigns. Analytics and performance tracking enable you to measure the effectiveness of your ads, gain insights into audience behavior, and make data-driven decisions to optimize future campaigns. This section will guide you through the key metrics to track, tools available for performance analysis, and strategies for leveraging this data to enhance your Facebook marketing efforts.

1. Key Metrics to Track

To evaluate the success of your Facebook ads, it's essential to monitor a range of key performance indicators (KPIs).

The primary metrics you should track:

1. Click-Through Rate (CTR)

CTR measures the percentage of people who clicked on your ad after seeing it. A high CTR indicates that your ad is relevant and engaging to your audience.

- **Formula:** CTR = (Clicks / Impressions) x 100

2. Conversion Rate

Conversion rate measures the percentage of users who completed a desired action (e.g., making a purchase, signing up for a newsletter) after clicking on your ad. This metric is crucial for understanding the effectiveness of your ad in driving specific outcomes.

- **Formula:** Conversion Rate = (Conversions / Clicks) x 100

3. Cost Per Click (CPC)

CPC measures the average amount you pay each time someone clicks on your ad. Monitoring CPC helps you manage your budget and optimize your ad spend.

- **Formula:** CPC = Total Spend / Total Clicks

4. Cost Per Acquisition (CPA)

CPA measures the average cost to acquire a new customer or lead. This metric is vital for assessing the profitability of your campaigns.

- **Formula:** CPA = Total Spend / Total Conversions

5. Return on Ad Spend (ROAS)

ROAS measures the revenue generated for every dollar spent on advertising. A high ROAS indicates that your ads are effectively driving revenue.

- **Formula:** ROAS = Revenue / Total Spend

6. Engagement Metrics

Engagement metrics include likes, shares, comments, and video views. High engagement levels indicate that your content resonates with your audience and encourages interaction.

7. Reach and Impressions

- **Reach:** The number of unique users who saw your ad.
- **Impressions:** The total number of times your ad was displayed, including multiple views by the same user.

Monitoring reach and impressions helps you understand the visibility and frequency of your ads.

2. Tools for Performance Analysis

Facebook offers a range of tools to help you track and analyze the performance of your ads:

1. Facebook Ads Manager

Ads Manager is the primary tool for creating, managing, and analyzing your Facebook ad campaigns. It provides detailed insights into various metrics and allows you to generate customized reports.

Key Features:
- **Campaign Overview:** Get a high-level view of your campaigns, including spend, reach, and results.
- **Breakdown Options:** Analyze performance by demographics, placement, and time.
- **Custom Reports:** Create and save custom reports to track specific metrics relevant to your goals.

2. Facebook Analytics

Facebook Analytics offers in-depth insights into user behavior across your website, app, and Facebook page. It provides a comprehensive view of the customer journey and helps you understand how users interact with your business.

Key Features:
- **Funnels:** Visualize the steps users take before completing a desired action.
- **Cohort Analysis:** Track user behavior over time to identify trends and retention rates.
- **Cross-Platform Insights:** Analyze interactions across multiple channels and devices.

3. Facebook Pixel

Facebook Pixel is a piece of code that you add to your website to track visitor actions and measure the effectiveness of your ads. It allows you to create Custom Audiences, optimize for conversions, and retarget users.

Key Features:
- **Conversion Tracking:** Measure actions such as purchases, sign-ups, and page views.
- **Audience Building:** Create Custom and Lookalike Audiences based on website activity.
- **Ad Optimization:** Improve ad delivery by targeting users who are more likely to convert.

3. Strategies for Leveraging Analytics

1. Set Clear Goals and KPIs

Before launching your campaigns, define clear goals and the KPIs that will measure your success. Whether your objective is to increase sales, generate leads, or boost brand awareness, having specific targets will help you focus your analysis.

2. Regularly Monitor Performance

Consistently track your ad performance to identify trends and make timely adjustments. Regular monitoring allows you to spot underperforming ads and optimize them before they consume too much of your budget.

3. Analyze Audience Insights

Use the audience insights provided by Facebook to understand who is engaging with your ads. Analyzing demographics, interests, and behaviors can help you refine your targeting and create more relevant ads.

4. Conduct A/B Testing

As mentioned earlier, A/B testing is essential for determining what works best in your campaigns. Test different ad variations and analyze the results to continually improve your ad performance.

5. Optimize Ad Creative and Copy

Based on your performance data, optimize your ad creative and copy to enhance engagement and conversions. Experiment with different visuals, headlines, and CTAs to see what resonates most with your audience.

6. Adjust Bidding and Budgeting

Use your analytics to inform your bidding strategy and budget allocation. If certain ads or campaigns are performing exceptionally well, consider increasing their budget to maximize their impact.

7. Leverage Retargeting

Utilize Facebook Pixel to retarget users who have interacted with your website or ads but haven't converted. Retargeting allows you to re-engage potential customers and encourage them to complete their purchase.

Analytics and performance tracking are the backbone of successful Facebook marketing campaigns. By understanding key metrics, utilizing Facebook's analytical tools, and implementing data-driven strategies, you can optimize your ads for better performance and higher ROI. Continuously analyze and refine your campaigns to stay ahead of the competition and achieve your marketing goals.

Understanding Facebook Insights

Facebook Insights is a powerful analytics tool that provides detailed information about your Facebook Page's performance. It offers valuable data on audience demographics, engagement, reach, and more, enabling you to make informed decisions about your content and marketing strategies. This section will guide you through the key features of Facebook Insights and how to leverage them to enhance your Facebook marketing efforts.

1. Navigating Facebook Insights

To access Facebook Insights, follow these steps:

1. Go to Your Facebook Page: Navigate to the Facebook Page you manage.
2. Click on Insights: Located at the top of your Page, this will open the Insights dashboard.

The Insights dashboard is divided into several sections, each providing different metrics and data about your Page's performance.

2. Key Features of Facebook Insights

1. Overview

The Overview section provides a snapshot of your Page's performance over the past seven days. It includes metrics such as:

- **Page Views:** The number of times your Page was viewed.
- **Page Likes:** The number of new likes your Page received.
- **Post Reach:** The number of people who saw your posts.
- **Post Engagement:** The number of reactions, comments, shares, and clicks your posts received.

2. Promotions

This section shows the performance of any paid promotions or boosted posts. It includes metrics such as reach, engagement, and the amount spent on each promotion.

3. Followers

The Followers section provides data on your Page's followers, including:

- **Total Followers:** The total number of people following your Page.
- **Net Followers:** The difference between new followers and unfollows over a specified period.
- **Follower Demographics:** Information about the age, gender, and location of your followers.

4. Likes

The Likes section offers insights into your Page's likes, including:

- **Total Page Likes:** The total number of likes your Page has received.

- **Net Likes:** The difference between new likes and unlikes over a specified period.
- **Source of Likes:** Information about where your likes are coming from (e.g., Page suggestions, ads).

5. Reach

The Reach section provides data on how many people saw your content and how they interacted with it. Key metrics include:

- **Post Reach:** The number of people who saw your posts.
- **Page Views:** The number of times your Page was viewed.
- **Page Previews:** The number of times people hovered over your Page name or profile picture to see a preview of your content.
- **Engagement:** The number of reactions, comments, shares, and clicks on your posts.

6. Page Views

This section provides detailed information about the number of views your Page received and where they came from. It includes:

- **Total Views:** The total number of times your Page was viewed.
- **Top Sources:** The top sources of traffic to your Page (e.g., Facebook search, external websites).

7. Actions on Page

The Actions on Page section tracks the actions people take on your Page, such as:

- **Clicks on Contact Info:** The number of clicks on your contact information (e.g., phone number, email).
- **Clicks on Call-to-Action (CTA) Button:** The number of clicks on your CTA button.
- **Clicks on Website Link:** The number of clicks on the link to your website.

8. Posts

The Posts section offers detailed insights into the performance of your individual posts. Key metrics include:

- **Post Reach:** The number of people who saw your post.
- **Post Engagement:** The number of reactions, comments, shares, and clicks on your post.
- **Best Time to Post:** Data on when your followers are most active, helping you optimize your posting schedule.

9. Events

If you host events on your Page, this section provides data on their performance, including:

- **Event Reach:** The number of people who saw your event.
- **Event Engagement:** The number of responses (interested, going) and interactions (likes, comments, shares) on your event.

10. Videos

The Videos section provides insights into the performance of your video content, including:

- **Video Views:** The number of times your videos were viewed for at least three seconds.
- **10-Second Views:** The number of times your videos were viewed for at least 10 seconds.
- **Top Videos:** The most viewed videos on your Page.

11. People

The People section offers demographic information about the people who like your Page, follow your Page, and engage with your content. This includes:

- **Age and Gender:** The age and gender breakdown of your audience.
- **Location:** The top cities and countries where your audience is located.
- **Language:** The primary languages spoken by your audience.

3. Leveraging Facebook Insights for Better Marketing

1. Understand Your Audience

Use the demographic data in the People section to gain a deeper understanding of your audience. Tailor your content and ads to match the interests, preferences, and behaviors of your audience segments.

2. Optimize Your Content Strategy

Analyze the performance of your posts in the Posts section to identify what type of content resonates most with your audience. Use this data to create more of what works and less of what doesn't.

3. Improve Engagement

Track engagement metrics in the Reach and Posts sections to see which posts generate the most interactions. Experiment with different types of content (e.g., images, videos, links) to boost engagement.

4. Maximize Reach

Monitor the Reach section to understand how far your content is spreading. Use this data to adjust your posting schedule, boost high-performing posts, and refine your targeting.

5. Enhance Video Strategy

If you use videos, the Videos section can help you understand what type of video content works best. Focus on creating videos that capture attention within the first few seconds to increase view duration and engagement.

6. Track Ad Performance

Use the Promotions section to measure the effectiveness of your paid campaigns. Adjust your ad creative, targeting, and budget based on the performance data to improve ROI.

7. Optimize Posting Times

The Posts section provides insights into when your audience is most active. Schedule your posts during these peak times to maximize visibility and engagement.

8. Analyze Event Success

If you host events, use the Events section to track their performance. Use the data to improve future events, increase attendance, and boost engagement.

Facebook Insights is an invaluable tool for understanding your audience, measuring your Page's performance, and optimizing your content strategy. By regularly analyzing the data provided by Facebook Insights, you can make informed decisions that enhance your Facebook marketing efforts and drive better results.

Key Metrics to Monitor

Monitoring key metrics is crucial for evaluating the effectiveness of your Facebook marketing efforts. Here are some key metrics to keep an eye on:

1. Reach: This metric measures the number of unique users who have seen your content. It provides insights into your content's visibility and potential audience size.

2. Engagement: Engagement metrics, such as likes, comments, shares, and clicks, indicate how your audience is interacting with your content. Higher engagement levels generally indicate that your content is resonating with your audience.

3. Click-Through Rate (CTR): CTR measures the percentage of people who clicked on your ad after seeing it. A high CTR indicates that your ad is compelling and relevant to your audience.

4. Conversion Rate: Conversion rate measures the percentage of users who completed a desired action after clicking on your ad, such as making a purchase or signing up for a newsletter. It provides insights into the effectiveness of your ad in driving conversions.

5. Cost Per Click (CPC): CPC measures the average cost you pay each time someone clicks on your ad. Monitoring CPC helps you manage your budget and optimize your ad spend.

6. Return on Ad Spend (ROAS): ROAS measures the revenue generated for every dollar spent on advertising. A high ROAS indicates that your ads are generating positive returns and driving profitable outcomes.

7. Audience Demographics: Understanding the demographics of your audience, such as age, gender, location, and interests, helps you tailor your content and targeting strategies to better reach and engage with your target audience.

8. Page Likes/Followers: Tracking the growth of your page likes or followers over time provides insights into the popularity and reach of your page.

9. Post Performance: Analyzing the performance of your individual posts, including reach, engagement, and clicks, helps you identify what type of content resonates most with your audience.

10. Ad Performance: Monitoring metrics such as ad impressions, clicks, CTR, and conversion rate helps you evaluate the effectiveness of your ad campaigns and optimize them for better results.

By regularly monitoring these key metrics, you can gain valuable insights into the performance of your Facebook marketing efforts and make data-driven decisions to optimize your strategies for success.

Using Data to Improve Your Strategy

Utilizing data to improve your Facebook marketing strategy is essential for maximizing your results and achieving your business objectives.

How you can leverage data effectively:

1. Analyzing Audience Insights: Dive into the demographic data provided by Facebook Insights to understand who your audience is. Use this information to tailor your content and targeting strategies to better reach and engage with your target audience.

2. Identifying High-Performing Content: Analyze the performance of your posts to identify what type of content resonates most with your audience. Look for patterns in engagement metrics such as likes, comments, shares, and clicks to determine which posts are generating the most engagement.

3. Optimizing Posting Times: Use insights from Facebook Insights to determine when your audience is most active. Schedule your posts during these peak times to maximize visibility and engagement.

4. Testing and Iterating: Experiment with different types of content, ad formats, targeting options, and messaging to see what works best for your audience. Continuously monitor the performance of your campaigns and make data-driven adjustments to optimize your strategy over time.

5. A/B Testing: Conduct A/B tests to compare different variables, such as ad creative, copy, targeting options, and bidding strategies. Analyze the results to identify the most effective approaches and refine your strategy accordingly.

6. Tracking Conversions: Set up conversion tracking to measure the effectiveness of your Facebook ads in driving desired actions, such as purchases, sign-ups, or downloads. Use this data to optimize your campaigns for better ROI.

7. Monitoring Ad Performance: Regularly monitor key metrics such as ad impressions, clicks, click-through rate (CTR), conversion rate, and cost per acquisition (CPA) to assess the performance of your Facebook ad campaigns. Adjust your targeting, bidding, and ad creative based on the insights gathered.

8. Using Retargeting: Utilize Facebook Pixel to retarget users who have interacted with your website or ads but haven't converted. Tailor your messaging to these audiences to encourage them to take the desired action.

9. Analyzing Competitor Insights: Keep an eye on your competitors' Facebook Pages and ads to gain insights into their strategies and performance. Identify opportunities and areas for improvement based on what's working well for them.

10. Staying Informed: Stay up-to-date with the latest trends, best practices, and changes in the Facebook algorithm to ensure that your strategy remains effective and competitive.

By harnessing the power of data and insights, you can continuously optimize your Facebook marketing strategy to drive better results and achieve your business goals.

Reporting and Presenting Results

Reporting and presenting results effectively is crucial for demonstrating the impact of your Facebook marketing efforts and gaining buy-in from stakeholders.

How you can create insightful and compelling reports:

1. Define Goals and KPIs: Start by clearly defining the goals of your Facebook marketing campaigns and the key performance indicators (KPIs) you'll use to measure success. Align these goals with your overall business objectives to ensure relevance.

2. Choose the Right Metrics: Select metrics that are meaningful and relevant to your goals. Focus on metrics such as reach, engagement, conversion rate, return on ad spend (ROAS), and cost per acquisition (CPA) to provide a comprehensive view of your performance.

3. Use Visualizations: Present data using visualizations such as charts, graphs, and tables to make it easier to understand and interpret. Visuals can help highlight trends, patterns, and insights more effectively than raw data alone.

4. Provide Context: Contextualize your data by providing explanations, insights, and analysis. Help stakeholders understand the significance of the results and how they relate to broader business objectives.

5. Include Comparative Analysis: Compare current performance with historical data or benchmarks to provide context and highlight progress over time. Use comparative analysis to identify areas of improvement and opportunities for growth.

6. Segmentation and Targeting Insights: Break down your data by audience segments, demographics, interests, or other relevant factors to provide deeper insights into audience behavior and preferences.

7. Highlight Success Stories: Showcase successful campaigns, case studies, or testimonials to demonstrate the impact of your Facebook marketing efforts. Use real-world examples to illustrate how your strategies have achieved tangible results.

8. Provide Recommendations: Based on your analysis, offer actionable recommendations for optimization and improvement. Highlight opportunities for refinement, expansion, or innovation to drive even better results in the future.

9. Keep it Concise and Relevant: Focus on presenting the most relevant and impactful information. Avoid overwhelming stakeholders with too much data or unnecessary details. Keep your reports concise, clear, and focused on the key takeaways.

10. Tailor to the Audience: Customize your reports to meet the needs and preferences of your audience. Present information in a format and style that resonates with stakeholders, whether it's a detailed written report, a visual presentation, or a live demonstration.

11. Schedule Regular Updates: Establish a cadence for reporting and communicate regularly with stakeholders. Schedule periodic updates to review performance, discuss insights, and make adjustments to your strategy as needed.

12. Encourage Discussion and Feedback: Foster open communication and collaboration by inviting stakeholders to ask questions, share insights, and provide feedback. Create a supportive environment where ideas can be exchanged and decisions can be made collaboratively.

By following these best practices for reporting and presenting results, you can effectively communicate the impact of your Facebook marketing efforts and build support for future initiatives.

Chapter 5: Advanced Strategies for Facebook Success

As you become more proficient with Facebook marketing, it's essential to delve into advanced strategies that can elevate your efforts and maximize your success. These strategies focus on sophisticated techniques and tools that can drive better engagement, more precise targeting, and higher conversions. Here's a comprehensive guide to advanced strategies for Facebook success.

1. Leveraging Facebook Pixel for Remarketing

What is Facebook Pixel?
Facebook Pixel is a piece of code that you place on your website to track conversions, optimize ads, build targeted audiences, and remarket to people who have interacted with your site.

Benefits of Facebook Pixel:

- **Conversion Tracking:** Measure the effectiveness of your ads by understanding the actions people take on your website.
- **Audience Building:** Create custom audiences based on website visitors and their actions.
- **Ad Optimization:** Improve ad performance by targeting users who are more likely to convert.

How to Implement Facebook Pixel:
1. **Set Up Facebook Pixel:** Go to the Events Manager in Facebook Ads Manager and create a Pixel.
2. **Install the Pixel Code:** Copy the Pixel code and place it in the header of your website.
3. **Track Events:** Set up standard and custom events to track specific actions like purchases, sign-ups, or page views.

2. Utilizing Lookalike Audiences

What are Lookalike Audiences?
Lookalike Audiences allow you to reach new people who are likely to be interested in your business

because they resemble your best existing customers.

Creating Lookalike Audiences:
1. Source Audience: Choose a source audience, such as a custom audience created from your customer list, website visitors, or app users.
2. Audience Size: Select the size of the Lookalike Audience. A smaller percentage will closely match your source audience, while a larger percentage will provide a broader reach.
3. Targeting: Use Lookalike Audiences in your ad campaigns to find new potential customers similar to your existing ones.

3. Advanced Targeting Options

Custom Audiences:
- **Website Traffic:** Target users who have visited your website.
- **Customer List:** Upload a list of your customers and target them with specific ads.
- **App Activity:** Target users based on their interactions with your app.

Behavioral and Demographic Targeting:
- **Interests and Behaviors:** Target users based on their interests, behaviors, and activities on Facebook.
- **Demographics:** Refine your audience based on demographics such as age, gender, education, and more.

4. Crafting High-Converting Ad Creative

Ad Formats:
- **Carousel Ads:** Showcase multiple images or videos in a single ad.
- **Collection Ads:** Feature a primary video or image with four smaller accompanying images in a grid layout.
- **Instant Experience:** Create immersive, fullscreen experiences that load instantly when someone taps on your ad.

Creative Best Practices:
- **Compelling Visuals:** Use high-quality images and videos that capture attention.

- **Clear Call-to-Action (CTA):** Include a strong CTA that tells users exactly what you want them to do.
- **Mobile Optimization:** Ensure your ads are optimized for mobile viewing.

5. Advanced Analytics and Performance Tracking

Using Facebook Analytics:
- **Funnel Analysis:** Understand the customer journey by analyzing how users move through your sales funnel.
- **Cohort Analysis:** Track the behavior of specific groups of users over time to identify trends and opportunities.

Third-Party Tools:
- **Google Analytics:** Integrate with Facebook Pixel to gain deeper insights into user behavior on your website.
- **Social Media Management Tools:** Use tools like Hootsuite, Sprout Social, or Buffer for

comprehensive social media analytics and reporting.

6. Automation and Scheduling

Automated Rules:
- **Set Up Automated Rules:** Create rules to automatically adjust your ad budgets, bids, and schedules based on performance metrics.
- **Examples of Rules:** Increase budget by 20% if the cost per conversion is below a certain threshold, or pause ads if the click-through rate drops below a specific percentage.

Scheduling Posts and Ads:
- **Content Calendar:** Plan and schedule your posts in advance using tools like Buffer or Hootsuite.
- **Ad Scheduling:** Run your ads during peak times when your target audience is most active.

7. A/B Testing and Experimentation

Importance of A/B Testing:

A/B testing allows you to compare two versions of an ad to see which performs better, helping you make data-driven decisions.

How to Conduct A/B Testing:
1. Choose a Variable: Test one variable at a time, such as ad copy, headline, image, or CTA.
2. Create Variations: Create two or more versions of the ad with the variable changed.
3. Run the Test: Run the ads simultaneously and track their performance.
4. Analyze Results: Determine which version performed better and use those insights to optimize future campaigns.

8. Exploring New Features and Trends

Stay Updated:
- **Facebook Business Blog:** Regularly check the Facebook Business Blog for updates on new features and best practices.
- **Industry News:** Follow industry news and trends to stay ahead of the curve and incorporate the latest strategies into your campaigns.

Experiment with New Features:
- **Facebook Stories:** Use Facebook Stories to create engaging, ephemeral content.
- **Messenger Bots:** Implement Messenger bots to automate customer service and engage with users in real-time.

By implementing these advanced strategies, you can enhance your Facebook marketing efforts, drive better results, and stay ahead of the competition. Continuously analyze your performance, experiment with new techniques, and optimize your approach to achieve long-term success on Facebook.

Leveraging Facebook Groups for Engagement

Facebook Groups are a powerful tool for building a community, fostering engagement, and creating meaningful interactions with your audience. Unlike Pages, which are often used for broadcasting information, Groups are designed for interaction and discussion.

How to effectively leverage Facebook Groups to enhance your marketing strategy:

1. Understanding the Value of Facebook Groups

Community Building: Groups allow you to create a sense of community around your brand, product, or interest. Members can interact with each other, share experiences, and offer support.

Engagement: Groups tend to have higher engagement rates compared to Pages. Members of a Group are more likely to see and interact with your posts.

Customer Insights: Groups provide valuable insights into your audience's interests, concerns, and feedback, which can inform your marketing strategy.

2. Setting Up Your Facebook Group

Define Your Purpose: Clearly define the purpose of your Group. Whether it's for customer support, brand advocacy, or niche interest, having a clear purpose will attract the right members.

Choose Privacy Settings:
- **Public:** Anyone can see the Group, its members, and their posts.
- **Closed:** Anyone can find the Group and see who's in it, but only members can see posts.
- **Secret:** Only members can find the Group and see posts.

Create Group Rules: Establish clear rules to ensure a positive and respectful environment. Rules help manage expectations and maintain the Group's focus.

Customize Your Group: Add a cover photo, description, and tags to make your Group attractive and easy to find.

3. Growing Your Group

Invite Your Audience: Invite your existing customers, followers, and email subscribers to join your Group. Promote your Group on your Facebook Page, website, and other social media platforms.

Collaborate with Influencers: Partner with influencers in your industry to promote your Group. Influencers can bring their followers into your community, expanding your reach.

Engage New Members: Welcome new members with a personalized message or post. Encourage them to introduce themselves and share their interests.

4. Creating Engaging Content

Discussion Starters: Post open-ended questions to spark discussions. Encourage members to share their opinions, experiences, and advice.

Polls and Surveys: Use polls and surveys to gather feedback and insights from your members.

This can help you understand their needs and preferences.

Exclusive Content: Share exclusive content such as behind-the-scenes looks, early access to new products, and special offers. This makes members feel valued and appreciated.

Live Videos and Q&A Sessions: Host live videos and Q&A sessions to engage with your members in real-time. This helps build a personal connection and trust.

User-Generated Content: Encourage members to share their own content related to your brand or industry. Highlight and celebrate their contributions to foster a sense of community.

5. Moderating and Managing Your Group

Active Moderation: Regularly monitor posts and comments to ensure they align with your Group's rules. Address any issues or conflicts promptly and fairly.

Promote Positive Interactions: Recognize and reward positive contributions from members. This can be through shoutouts, badges, or other forms of recognition.

Use Moderation Tools: Utilize Facebook's moderation tools such as keyword alerts, post approval settings, and member management options to streamline your moderation efforts.

6. Analyzing Group Performance

Group Insights: Use Facebook's Group Insights to track key metrics such as member growth, engagement, and popular posts. This data helps you understand what's working and where you can improve.

Feedback from Members: Regularly solicit feedback from your members to understand their needs and expectations. Use this feedback to make informed decisions about the direction of your Group.

Adjust Your Strategy: Based on your analysis, continuously refine your content and engagement strategies. Experiment with different types of posts and activities to see what resonates best with your members.

7. Integrating Groups with Your Overall Marketing Strategy

Cross-Promote Content: Share relevant content from your Facebook Page, blog, or other social media channels in your Group. Conversely, share engaging discussions and posts from your Group on your other platforms.

Drive Traffic to Your Website: Use your Group to drive traffic to your website by sharing links to blog posts, product pages, and other relevant content.

Leverage Group Insights for Product Development: Use the insights and feedback gathered from your Group to inform your product development and marketing strategies.

Understanding your community's needs can lead to better products and services.

By leveraging Facebook Groups effectively, you can create a thriving community that fosters engagement, builds loyalty, and drives meaningful interactions with your brand. Continuously nurture your Group, listen to your members, and adapt your strategies to ensure long-term success.

Influencer Partnerships and Collaborations

Influencer partnerships and collaborations can significantly enhance your Facebook marketing strategy by leveraging the reach and credibility of individuals who have a strong following.

How to effectively use influencer partnerships to boost your brand's presence on Facebook.

1. Understanding the Benefits of Influencer Partnerships

Extended Reach: Influencers have established audiences that trust their recommendations. Collaborating with them can introduce your brand to a larger and more diverse audience.

Credibility and Trust: Influencers are seen as authentic and trustworthy by their followers. Their endorsement can add credibility to your brand and products.

Targeted Audience: Influencers often have niche audiences that align with specific interests or demographics. This allows you to reach a highly targeted audience that is more likely to be interested in your offerings.

Engagement: Influencers typically have high engagement rates. Their followers are more likely to interact with content that features the influencer, resulting in better engagement for your brand.

2. Finding the Right Influencers

Define Your Goals: Determine what you want to achieve with your influencer partnerships. Whether it's increasing brand awareness, driving sales, or growing your social media following, your goals will guide your influencer selection.

Research and Identify Influencers:
- **Relevance:** Look for influencers whose content aligns with your brand values and target audience.
- **Reach:** Consider the size of the influencer's following. While larger followings can offer more exposure, micro-influencers (with smaller, highly engaged audiences) can also be very effective.
- **Engagement:** Analyze the influencer's engagement rates, including likes, comments, and shares. High engagement indicates an active and interested audience.

Tools for Finding Influencers: Use tools like Influencity, BuzzSumo, and HypeAuditor to discover and evaluate potential influencers based on their reach, engagement, and audience demographics.

3. Building Relationships with Influencers

Engage with Their Content: Start by following the influencers you're interested in and engaging with their content. Comment on their posts, share their content, and show genuine interest in their work.

Personalized Outreach: When reaching out to influencers, personalize your message. Mention specific posts or campaigns of theirs that you admire and explain why you think a collaboration would be mutually beneficial.

Offer Value: Clearly outline what you can offer the influencer in return for their partnership. This could be monetary compensation, free products, exclusive access, or exposure to your audience.

4. Collaborating with Influencers

Define the Collaboration Scope: Clearly define the scope of the collaboration. What type of content will be created? How often will it be posted? What are the key messages and calls to action?

Content Creation: Allow influencers creative freedom to create content that resonates with their audience while aligning with your brand guidelines. Authenticity is key to successful influencer marketing.

Campaign Integration: Integrate influencer content with your broader marketing campaigns. Share their posts on your own social media channels and website to maximize exposure.

Use Branded Content Tools: Utilize Facebook's branded content tools to tag partnerships in posts. This increases transparency and allows you to track the performance of influencer content.

5. Measuring the Success of Influencer Campaigns

Set Clear Metrics: Establish clear metrics to measure the success of your influencer campaigns. These could include reach, engagement, website traffic, conversions, and ROI.

Monitor Performance: Use Facebook Insights and other analytics tools to monitor the performance of influencer posts. Track key metrics such as likes, comments, shares, and click-through rates.

Gather Feedback: Collect feedback from influencers and their followers to understand what worked well and what could be improved. This can provide valuable insights for future campaigns.

Analyze Results: Compare the results against your initial goals. Identify the aspects of the campaign that were most successful and those that need refinement.

6. Building Long-Term Partnerships

Nurture Relationships: Building long-term relationships with influencers can lead to more authentic and impactful collaborations. Stay in touch with influencers and engage with their content even when you're not actively running a campaign.

Exclusive Collaborations: Offer influencers exclusive opportunities to work with your brand. This can make them feel valued and more invested in your brand's success.

Feedback and Iteration: Continuously seek feedback from your influencer partners and iterate on your strategies. Collaborative relationships should evolve based on mutual learning and growth.

By effectively leveraging influencer partnerships and collaborations, you can significantly enhance your brand's presence and engagement on Facebook. These partnerships not only extend your reach but also build trust and credibility with your target audience, driving long-term success for your marketing efforts.

Running Contests and Giveaways

Contests and giveaways are powerful tools for boosting engagement, increasing your reach, and growing your audience on Facebook. When executed correctly, they can generate excitement, foster community, and create positive associations with your brand. Here's how to effectively run contests and giveaways on Facebook.

1. Setting Clear Objectives

Define Your Goals: Before launching a contest or giveaway, clearly define your objectives. Are you aiming to increase brand awareness, grow your follower count, drive traffic to your website, or generate user-generated content? Your goals will shape the structure and rules of your contest.

2. Choosing the Right Type of Contest or Giveaway

Types of Contests:

- **Like and Share:** Encourage users to like and share your post to enter the contest. This increases visibility and reach.
- **Comment to Win:** Ask users to comment on your post to participate. This drives engagement and sparks conversation.
- **Photo/Video Contests:** Invite users to submit photos or videos related to your brand or theme. This generates user-generated content and fosters creativity.
- **Tag a Friend:** Encourage users to tag friends in the comments. This expands your audience and can attract new followers.

Types of Giveaways:
- **Random Draw:** Select a winner at random from all entries. This is simple and fair.
- **Contest-Based:** Choose a winner based on the quality or creativity of their entry. This encourages higher-quality submissions but requires more effort to judge.

3. Planning and Preparing Your Contest or Giveaway

Define the Prize: Choose a prize that is appealing to your target audience. It should be valuable enough to motivate participation but relevant to your brand.

Set the Rules: Clearly outline the rules, including how to enter, eligibility criteria, start and end dates, and how the winner will be chosen. Ensure your rules comply with Facebook's guidelines and any legal requirements in your region.

Create Engaging Graphics and Copy: Design eye-catching visuals and write compelling copy to promote your contest. Highlight the prize and how to enter, and include a clear call to action.

Develop a Promotion Plan: Plan how you will promote your contest. Use your Facebook Page, Facebook Ads, email newsletters, and other social media platforms to spread the word.

4. Launching and Managing Your Contest or Giveaway

Post the Contest Announcement: Publish your contest announcement post with all the necessary details. Pin the post to the top of your Page to ensure it's easily accessible.

Engage with Participants: Interact with participants by liking and replying to their comments. This builds community and encourages more participation.

Monitor Entries: Keep track of entries and ensure they comply with the contest rules. Use tools like spreadsheets or contest management software to organize and manage entries.

5. Selecting and Announcing the Winner

Random Draw Tools: If you're running a random draw, use tools like Random.org to ensure a fair and transparent selection process.

Judging Criteria: For contest-based giveaways, assemble a panel of judges and establish clear criteria for evaluating entries. Ensure the judging process is fair and unbiased.

Announce the Winner: Publicly announce the winner on your Facebook Page. Celebrate their win with a congratulatory post and ask them to contact you via direct message to claim their prize.

6. Post-Contest Follow-Up

Thank Participants: Thank all participants for entering and engaging with your contest. Express your appreciation and invite them to stay connected with your brand.

Share User-Generated Content: If your contest generated user content, share some of the best entries on your Facebook Page (with permission). This showcases your community's creativity and provides additional content.

Analyze the Results: Evaluate the success of your contest based on your initial objectives. Analyze metrics such as reach, engagement, new followers, and website traffic to measure the impact.

Gather Feedback: Ask participants for feedback on the contest experience. Use their insights to improve future contests and giveaways.

7. Best Practices and Legal Considerations

Follow Facebook's Guidelines: Ensure your contest complies with Facebook's promotion policies. You must include a disclaimer stating that the promotion is not sponsored, endorsed, or administered by Facebook.

Legal Compliance: Be aware of legal requirements related to contests and giveaways in your region. This may include rules about age restrictions, eligibility, and prize distribution.

Clear Communication: Communicate clearly and transparently throughout the contest. Ensure participants understand the rules, how winners will be chosen, and when the winner will be announced.

Fairness and Integrity: Maintain fairness and integrity throughout the contest. Avoid any practices that could be perceived as favoritism or manipulation.

By running well-organized and engaging contests and giveaways, you can significantly boost your brand's visibility, foster community engagement, and achieve your marketing goals on Facebook.

Integrating Facebook with Other Marketing Channels

Integrating Facebook with your other marketing channels can create a cohesive and comprehensive strategy that maximizes your reach and impact. By leveraging the strengths of each platform and ensuring consistency in your messaging, you can enhance your overall marketing efforts. Here's how to effectively integrate Facebook with other marketing channels.

1. Understanding the Importance of Integration

Consistency in Branding: Ensure your brand's voice, visuals, and messaging are consistent across all channels to create a unified brand experience.

Enhanced Reach: Different channels can reach different segments of your audience. Integrating them ensures you cover a broader audience.

Increased Engagement: Cross-promotion encourages your audience to engage with you on multiple platforms, increasing overall engagement and loyalty.

Improved Analytics: Integrated campaigns provide a holistic view of performance, helping you understand how each channel contributes to your marketing goals.

2. Email Marketing Integration

Promote Your Facebook Page: Include links to your Facebook Page in your email newsletters. Encourage subscribers to follow you for more updates and exclusive content.

Use Facebook for Email Sign-Ups: Use Facebook ads to drive traffic to your email sign-up page. Offer incentives like exclusive content or discounts for new subscribers.

Sync Email and Facebook Campaigns: Align your email campaigns with your Facebook content calendar. Promote similar themes and campaigns simultaneously for cohesive messaging.

Custom Audiences from Email Lists: Upload your email list to Facebook to create custom audiences. This allows you to retarget your email subscribers with specific ads, increasing the relevance and effectiveness of your campaigns.

3. Website and Blog Integration

Social Sharing Buttons: Add Facebook sharing buttons to your website and blog posts to make it easy for visitors to share your content on their Facebook profiles.

Facebook Pixel: Install the Facebook Pixel on your website to track visitor behavior, optimize ads, and create custom audiences based on website interactions.

Embedded Posts and Widgets: Embed Facebook posts, videos, or widgets on your website to showcase your social media content and encourage website visitors to follow you on Facebook.

Promote Website Content on Facebook: Share blog posts, product pages, and other valuable content from your website on your Facebook Page to drive traffic and increase engagement.

4. Cross-Promoting on Other Social Media Platforms

Consistent Branding: Maintain a consistent brand identity across all social media platforms. Use similar profile pictures, cover photos, and bio descriptions.

Cross-Promotional Posts: Share content from your Facebook Page on other social media platforms like Instagram, Twitter, and LinkedIn. Encourage your followers on these platforms to connect with you on Facebook as well.

Unified Campaigns: Run integrated campaigns across multiple social media platforms. Use platform-specific features to tailor your message while maintaining a cohesive overall theme.

Social Media Contests and Challenges: Create contests or challenges that require participation on multiple platforms. This encourages your audience to engage with you across different channels.

5. Integrating with Paid Advertising

Retargeting Campaigns: Use Facebook Pixel to retarget website visitors with ads on Facebook. This keeps your brand top-of-mind and encourages conversions.

Multi-Platform Ad Campaigns: Run ad campaigns that span multiple platforms, including Facebook, Instagram, Google Ads, and LinkedIn. Coordinate your messaging and visuals for a unified approach.

Custom Audiences and Lookalikes: Use data from your other marketing channels to create custom and lookalike audiences on Facebook. This enhances targeting precision and improves ad performance.

6. Offline Marketing Integration

Promote Social Media Offline: Include your Facebook handle and a call-to-action on print materials, business cards, in-store signage, and product packaging.

Events and Trade Shows: Use Facebook to promote offline events and encourage attendees to follow your Page for updates. During the event, encourage live social media engagement with hashtags and live streaming.

QR Codes: Use QR codes on offline materials that link directly to your Facebook Page or specific posts. This provides an easy way for people to connect with you online.

7. Leveraging Influencers and Partnerships

Cross-Promote with Influencers: Collaborate with influencers to promote your Facebook content on their other social media channels. This can help attract new followers and increase engagement.

Partnership Campaigns: Work with other brands to create joint campaigns that leverage both of your audiences. Promote each other's Facebook Pages and content for mutual benefit.

8. Utilizing Analytics for Integration

Unified Dashboard: Use tools like Google Analytics, Hootsuite, or Sprout Social to create a unified dashboard that tracks performance across all channels. This helps you understand how each channel contributes to your overall strategy.

Cross-Channel Insights: Analyze data from all your marketing channels to gain insights into audience behavior and preferences. Use these insights to optimize your content and campaigns across all platforms.

Attribution Modeling: Implement attribution modeling to understand the customer journey and the role each channel plays in conversions. This helps you allocate resources more effectively.

By integrating Facebook with your other marketing channels, you can create a seamless and powerful marketing strategy that maximizes your reach, engagement, and conversions. Consistent messaging, cross-promotion, and data-driven insights are key to achieving a cohesive and effective marketing approach.

Staying Ahead of Facebook Algorithm Changes

Facebook's algorithm is constantly evolving to improve user experience by prioritizing content that is most relevant and engaging. As a marketer, staying ahead of these changes is crucial for maintaining and growing your reach and engagement. Here's how to stay ahead of Facebook algorithm changes and ensure your content remains visible and impactful.

1. Understanding the Facebook Algorithm

Core Principles: Facebook's algorithm prioritizes content that sparks meaningful interactions. This means posts that generate comments, shares, and reactions are more likely to be seen by a broader audience.

Key Factors:

- **Engagement:** Posts that receive high engagement (likes, comments, shares) are prioritized.

- **Relevance:** Content that is relevant to the user's interests and past interactions is shown more frequently.

- **Timeliness:** Newer posts are often given more priority, although highly engaging older posts can still surface.

- **Content Type:** Different content types (videos, images, links) are weighted differently. Video content, especially live videos, tends to get more engagement and higher priority.

2. Creating High-Quality, Engaging Content

Focus on Quality: Ensure your content is valuable, informative, and entertaining to your audience. High-quality content naturally attracts more engagement.

Encourage Interaction: Ask questions, create polls, and prompt discussions to encourage comments and shares. The more interactions your post generates, the better its visibility.

Use Visuals: Posts with images and videos tend to perform better. Use high-quality visuals to capture attention and drive engagement.

Live Videos: Live streaming tends to get higher engagement rates. Use Facebook Live to connect with your audience in real-time, answer questions, and provide behind-the-scenes content.

3. Staying Informed About Algorithm Changes

Follow Facebook News: Keep up with announcements from Facebook's official blog and news sections. This is where major updates and changes to the algorithm are often first reported.

Join Industry Groups: Participate in marketing and social media groups on Facebook and LinkedIn. These communities are quick to discuss and analyze new changes, providing valuable insights and tips.

Subscribe to Newsletters: Sign up for newsletters from social media experts and agencies. They often provide analysis and updates on platform changes, including Facebook's algorithm.

Attend Webinars and Conferences: Participate in digital marketing webinars and conferences. These events often feature sessions on the latest trends and updates in social media algorithms.

4. Utilizing Facebook Insights and Analytics

Monitor Engagement: Regularly review your Page Insights to understand what types of content are performing best. Look for patterns in posts that get high engagement and replicate their success.

Track Key Metrics: Focus on metrics like reach, engagement rate, and click-through rates. These can give you a clear picture of how well your content is resonating with your audience.

Experiment and Adapt: Test different types of content, posting times, and formats. Use the data from your experiments to refine your strategy and stay aligned with the algorithm's preferences.

5. Leveraging Paid Promotions

Boost High-Performing Posts: Identify posts that are already performing well organically and boost them with paid promotion. This can increase their reach and engagement even further.

Targeted Ads: Use Facebook's advanced targeting options to reach specific audience segments. The more relevant your ads are to your audience, the better they will perform.

Retargeting Campaigns: Implement retargeting campaigns to re-engage users who have interacted with your content or visited your website. This keeps your brand top-of-mind and encourages further interaction.

6. Building a Community

Foster a Community: Create a sense of community on your Page by engaging with your audience. Respond to comments, ask for feedback, and show appreciation for your followers.

Facebook Groups: Consider creating or participating in Facebook Groups related to your industry or brand. Groups tend to have high engagement and can be a valuable way to build a community around your brand.

User-Generated Content: Encourage your audience to create content related to your brand. User-generated content not only provides social proof but also tends to get high engagement.

7. Avoiding Penalties and Ensuring Compliance

Avoid Clickbait: Facebook penalizes posts that use misleading headlines or sensationalized content to attract clicks. Ensure your content is honest and straightforward.

Follow Community Standards: Ensure your posts comply with Facebook's community standards and guidelines. Violations can lead to reduced reach or even account suspension.

Transparent Practices: Be transparent with your audience about promotions, sponsored content, and any contests or giveaways. Transparency builds trust and ensures compliance with Facebook's policies.

By staying informed and adaptive, you can navigate Facebook's algorithm changes effectively. Focus on creating engaging, high-quality content, leveraging insights, and building a strong community to ensure your brand continues to thrive on the platform.

Appendix

The appendix of "The Facebook Marketing Secrets Guide" provides additional resources, templates, and tools to enhance your understanding and execution of the strategies discussed in the book. Use this section as a reference for practical applications, further readings, and advanced tools.

Appendix A: Useful Tools and Resources

1. Social Media Management Tools
   - **Hootsuite:** A comprehensive tool for scheduling posts, monitoring social media channels, and analyzing performance.
   - **Buffer:** Simplifies content scheduling and provides insights on engagement metrics.
   - **Sprout Social:** Offers robust features for social media management, including analytics, engagement, and team collaboration.

2. Facebook Advertising Tools

- **Facebook Ads Manager:** The primary tool for creating, managing, and analyzing Facebook ad campaigns.

- **AdEspresso:** Simplifies the process of creating and optimizing Facebook ads with powerful analytics and split testing features.

- **PowerAdSpy:** Allows you to spy on your competitors' ads and find winning ad strategies.

3. Analytics and Reporting Tools

- **Google Analytics:** Integrate with Facebook to track website traffic and user behavior stemming from Facebook campaigns.

- **Klipfolio:** Create custom dashboards to monitor your social media performance across multiple platforms.

- **Cyfe:** An all-in-one business dashboard app that helps track multiple social media accounts and marketing campaigns.

4. Content Creation Tools

- **Canva:** A user-friendly design tool for creating visually appealing graphics and social media posts.

- **Adobe Spark:** Allows you to create stunning videos, graphics, and web pages with ease.

- **Piktochart:** Helps in creating engaging infographics and visual content.

5. Audience Research Tools

- **Facebook Audience Insights:** Provides detailed information about your target audience's demographics, interests, and behaviors.

- **BuzzSumo:** Identifies popular content and influencers within your industry.

- **SurveyMonkey:** Conduct surveys to gather insights directly from your audience.

Appendix B: Templates and Worksheets

1. Content Calendar Template

- A template to help you plan and schedule your Facebook posts. Includes columns for date, time, content type, post copy, visuals, and links.

2. Ad Campaign Planning Worksheet

- A worksheet to outline your ad campaign goals, target audience, budget, ad copy, visuals, and metrics for success.

3. Audience Persona Template

- Create detailed profiles of your target audience, including demographics, interests, pain points, and preferred content types.

4. Engagement Tracking Sheet

- Track your engagement metrics such as likes, comments, shares, and messages. Helps in identifying trends and optimizing your strategy.

5. Analytics Reporting Template

- A template to compile and present your social media analytics. Includes sections for reach, engagement, website traffic, and conversions.

Appendix C: Further Reading and Learning

1. Books

- **"Jab, Jab, Jab, Right Hook" by Gary Vaynerchuk:** A guide to creating compelling content for social media.

- **"Contagious: How to Build Word of Mouth in the Digital Age" by Jonah Berger:** Insights into why things catch on and how to make your content more shareable.

- **"Influence: The Psychology of Persuasion" by Robert B. Cialdini:** Understanding the principles of persuasion can help in crafting more effective marketing messages.

2. Online Courses

- **Facebook Blueprint:** Free courses and certifications offered by Facebook to help you master their advertising platform.

- **Coursera - Social Media Marketing Specialization:** A comprehensive course covering all aspects of social media marketing, including Facebook.

- **HubSpot Academy - Social Media Certification:** Free certification course covering various social media strategies and best practices.

3. Blogs and Websites

- **Social Media Examiner:** Offers articles, podcasts, and webinars on the latest social media marketing trends.

- **Buffer Blog:** Insights and tips on social media marketing, including Facebook strategies.

- **Neil Patel's Blog:** Comprehensive guides and tips on digital marketing, including social media strategies.

4. Industry Reports

- **Hootsuite's Social Media Trends Report:** Annual report detailing the latest trends in social media marketing.

- **Sprout Social Index:** Insights into social media trends and user behaviors.

- **We Are Social's Digital Report:** Comprehensive data on social media usage and trends globally.

Appendix D: Glossary of Key Terms

1. Algorithm: A set of rules that determines which content appears in a user's feed based on their behavior and interactions.

2. Engagement Rate: A metric that measures the level of interaction (likes, comments, shares) a piece of content receives relative to its reach.

3. Reach: The number of unique users who see your content.

4. CTR (Click-Through Rate): The percentage of users who click on a link or ad out of the total users who view it.

5. ROI (Return on Investment): A measure of the profitability of your marketing efforts, calculated by comparing the revenue generated to the cost of the campaign.

6. A/B Testing: A method of comparing two versions of a piece of content or ad to determine which performs better.

Appendix E: Case Studies and Success Stories

1. Case Study: Boosting Engagement with Video Content

- Overview of a brand that significantly increased engagement and reach by incorporating video content into their Facebook strategy.

2. Case Study: Successful Ad Campaign for a Product Launch

- Detailed analysis of a product launch campaign that utilized Facebook ads to achieve high conversion rates and sales.

3. Case Study: Building a Community through Facebook Groups

- Example of a company that created a highly engaged community using Facebook Groups, leading to increased brand loyalty and customer retention.

4. Case Study: Effective Use of Influencer Marketing

- Insights into a campaign that partnered with influencers to expand reach and generate buzz around a new product.

By utilizing the resources, templates, and insights provided in this appendix, you can effectively implement and enhance your Facebook marketing strategies.

Glossary of Facebook Marketing Terms

1. Algorithm: A set of rules used by Facebook to determine which content appears in a user's News Feed, based on factors like user interaction, relevance, and content type.

2. Boosted Post: A post that you pay to promote to a larger audience. Boosting a post increases its visibility and reach beyond your current followers.

3. Click-Through Rate (CTR): The percentage of people who click on a link or ad out of the total number of people who view it. It's calculated by dividing the number of clicks by the number of impressions and multiplying by 100.

4. Custom Audience: A specific group of people you can target with your ads. These audiences can be created using data from your website, customer lists, or app activity.

5. Engagement: Actions that users take on your content, such as likes, comments, shares, and reactions. High engagement typically indicates that your content is resonating with your audience.

6. Facebook Ads Manager: The tool provided by Facebook for creating, managing, and analyzing ad campaigns. It offers detailed targeting options, budget settings, and performance metrics.

7. Facebook Pixel: A piece of code that you place on your website to track conversions from Facebook ads, optimize ads, build targeted audiences, and retarget website visitors.

8. Lookalike Audience: An audience created by Facebook based on the characteristics of your existing custom audiences. It's used to find new potential customers who have similar interests and behaviors.

9. Organic Reach: The number of people who see your content without paid promotion. Organic reach is determined by the algorithm and can be influenced by engagement and content quality.

10. Paid Reach: The number of people who see your content as a result of paid promotions, such as boosted posts or ads.

11. Relevance Score: A metric that rates the quality and relevance of your ads to your target audience. A higher relevance score can lower your ad costs and improve performance.

12. Retargeting: A strategy that involves showing ads to people who have previously interacted with your website or content. Retargeting helps keep your brand top-of-mind and encourages conversions.

13. Return on Investment (ROI): A measure of the profitability of your marketing efforts, calculated by comparing the revenue generated from your campaigns to the cost of those campaigns.

14. Social Proof: The influence that the actions and behaviors of others have on your own behavior. In Facebook marketing, social proof can be seen in likes, comments, shares, and user-generated content.

15. Stories: A content format that allows users to share photos and videos that disappear after 24 hours. Stories are displayed at the top of the Facebook app and are designed for short, engaging content.

16. Targeting: The process of defining the specific audience you want to reach with your ads. Targeting options include demographics, interests, behaviors, and custom audiences.

17. Video Views: A metric that measures the number of times your video content is viewed.

Facebook provides detailed insights into video performance, including average watch time and audience retention.

18. Impressions: The number of times your content is displayed on users' screens. Impressions measure exposure but do not account for engagement.

19. Reach: The number of unique users who see your content. Reach can be organic or paid, depending on how the content is distributed.

20. Engagement Rate: The percentage of people who engage with your content (likes, comments, shares) out of the total number of people who see it. It's calculated by dividing total engagements by total reach and multiplying by 100.

21. User-Generated Content (UGC): Content created by your audience, such as photos, videos, and reviews, that you can share on your page. UGC can enhance credibility and foster community engagement.

22. Insights: The analytics provided by Facebook to help you understand the performance of your content and ads. Insights include metrics like reach, engagement, demographics, and more.

23. Conversion: A desired action that you want the user to take, such as making a purchase, signing up for a newsletter, or downloading a resource. Conversions are often tracked using the Facebook Pixel.

24. Cost Per Click (CPC): The amount you pay each time someone clicks on your ad. CPC is a common metric used in Facebook advertising to measure the efficiency of your ads.

25. Cost Per Thousand Impressions (CPM): The cost of showing your ad one thousand times. CPM is another metric used to measure the efficiency of your ad campaigns, particularly in brand awareness campaigns.

26. Frequency: The average number of times each person sees your ad. Monitoring frequency helps ensure that your audience is not being overexposed to the same ad.

27. Page Insights: Detailed analytics available to Facebook Page admins that provide information on page performance, audience demographics, and post engagement.

28. Ad Placement: The location where your ads appear on Facebook, including the News Feed, Stories, Marketplace, and the right column on the desktop. You can choose automatic placements or manually select placements.

29. Brand Awareness: A campaign objective focused on increasing recognition and familiarity with your brand. Facebook offers specific ad formats and metrics to support brand awareness goals.

30. Engagement Rate: A metric that measures the level of interaction (likes, comments, shares) a piece of content receives relative to its reach.

By familiarizing yourself with these key terms, you'll be better equipped to navigate Facebook marketing, optimize your strategies, and achieve your business goals.

Resources and Tools for Facebook Marketers

Facebook offers a variety of tools and resources to help marketers effectively manage their Facebook Pages, create engaging content, and run successful ad campaigns.

Here are some of the key resources and tools available:

1. Facebook Business Suite

- **Purpose:** Manage your Facebook and Instagram business accounts in one place, including scheduling posts, responding to messages, and viewing insights.
- **Key Features:** Post scheduling, inbox management, performance tracking, and ad management.
- **Access:** Available for free to all Facebook and Instagram business account owners.

2. Facebook Ads Manager

- **Purpose:** Create, manage, and track Facebook ad campaigns.
- **Key Features:** Ad creation, audience targeting, budget management, and performance tracking.
- **Access:** Available for free to all Facebook business account owners.

3. Facebook Page Insights

- **Purpose:** Gain insights into your Page's performance, including audience demographics, post reach, and engagement metrics.

- **Key Features:** Overview dashboard, post-level insights, audience demographics, and engagement metrics.
- **Access:** Available for free to all Facebook Page admins.

4. Facebook Creator Studio

- **Purpose:** Manage your Facebook and Instagram content, including posts, stories, and live videos.
- **Key Features:** Content scheduling, performance tracking, monetization tools, and rights management.
- **Access:** Available for free to all Facebook and Instagram business account owners.

5. Facebook Blueprint

- **Purpose:** Learn how to use Facebook's tools and ad products through online courses and certifications.
- **Key Features:** Courses on ad creation, targeting, measurement, and best practices.

- **Access:** Available for free to all Facebook advertisers and marketers.

6. Facebook Business Help Center

- **Purpose:** Access resources, articles, and guides to help you navigate Facebook's business tools and policies.
- **Key Features:** Articles on troubleshooting, best practices, and updates.
- **Access:** Available for free to all Facebook advertisers and marketers.

7. Facebook Groups

- **Purpose:** Join Facebook Groups related to marketing, advertising, and specific industries to network and learn from peers.
- **Key Features:** Discussion forums, networking opportunities, and access to industry experts.
- **Access:** Available for free to all Facebook users.

8. Facebook Ad Library

- **Purpose:** View active and inactive ads from any Facebook Page, including ad creative, targeting information, and engagement metrics.
- **Key Features:** Searchable database of ads, including ad spend ranges and impressions.
- **Access:** Available for free to all Facebook users.

9. Facebook Business Blog

- **Purpose:** Stay up-to-date with the latest news, updates, and tips from Facebook for businesses.
- **Key Features:** Articles on new features, case studies, and best practices.
- **Access:** Available for free to all Facebook advertisers and marketers.

10. Facebook Live Producer

- **Purpose:** Create and manage live video broadcasts on Facebook Pages and Profiles.
- **Key Features:** Live video streaming, interactive features, and performance tracking.
- **Access:** Available for free to all Facebook users with Pages or Profiles.

These resources and tools can help you effectively manage and optimize your Facebook marketing efforts, reach your target audience, and achieve your business goals.

Template: Facebook Marketing Plan

Creating a comprehensive Facebook marketing plan is essential for maximizing the impact of your social media efforts. Use this template to outline your strategy, set goals, and define tactics for achieving success on Facebook.

1. Executive Summary

- **Objective:** Summarize the purpose and goals of your Facebook marketing plan.
- **Key Points:** Highlight key strategies, target audience, and anticipated outcomes.

2. Business Overview

- **Mission Statement:** Define your company's mission and values.
- **Product/Service Overview:** Provide a brief description of your offerings.
- **Target Audience:** Describe your ideal customer demographics, interests, and behaviors.

3. Goals and Objectives

- **SMART Goals:** Define specific, measurable, achievable, relevant, and time-bound goals for your Facebook marketing efforts.
- **Examples:**
  - Increase brand awareness by X% in the next six months.
  - Generate X leads/sales from Facebook ads within the next quarter.

4. Audience Analysis

- **Primary Audience:** Describe your primary target audience in detail.

- **Secondary Audiences:** Identify any secondary audience segments you want to reach.
- **Audience Insights:** Utilize Facebook Audience Insights to gather demographic and behavioral data.

5. Content Strategy

- **Content Themes:** Define the key topics and themes for your Facebook content.
- **Content Types:** Determine the types of content you'll create, such as articles, videos, infographics, etc.
- **Content Calendar:** Develop a content calendar outlining the timing and frequency of your posts.

6. Engagement Strategy

- **Community Management:** Outline how you'll engage with your audience through comments, messages, and interactions.
- **User-Generated Content (UGC):** Encourage users to create and share content related to your brand.

- **Contests and Giveaways:** Plan occasional contests or giveaways to boost engagement and attract new followers.

7. Advertising Strategy

- **Ad Objectives:** Define the purpose of your Facebook ads (e.g., brand awareness, lead generation, conversions).
- **Targeting Strategy:** Specify the audience demographics, interests, and behaviors you'll target with your ads.
- **Ad Formats:** Determine which ad formats (e.g., carousel, video, lead form) are best suited to your objectives.

8. Measurement and Analytics

- **Key Metrics:** Identify the key performance indicators (KPIs) you'll use to measure success (e.g., reach, engagement, conversions).
- **Tracking Tools:** Set up Facebook Pixel and other tracking tools to monitor ad performance and website conversions.

- **Reporting Cadence:** Establish a schedule for analyzing data and generating reports on campaign performance.

9. Budget Allocation

- **Ad Budget:** Determine how much you'll allocate to Facebook advertising on a monthly or quarterly basis.
- **Campaign Budgets:** Break down your budget by campaign objective and allocate funds accordingly.
- **Testing Budget:** Allocate a portion of your budget for testing new strategies, ad formats, and targeting options.

10. Optimization and Iteration

- **Testing Plan:** Outline a plan for testing and optimizing your Facebook campaigns over time.
- **Iterative Approach:** Commit to regularly reviewing performance data and making adjustments based on insights.

- **Continuous Learning:** Stay informed about new Facebook features, trends, and best practices to inform your strategy.

11. Risk Management

- **Contingency Plans:** Identify potential risks or challenges that could impact your Facebook marketing efforts.
- **Mitigation Strategies:** Develop strategies for mitigating risks and addressing issues as they arise.
- **Crisis Communication:** Establish protocols for responding to negative feedback or PR crises on Facebook.

12. Timeline and Milestones

- **Implementation Timeline:** Create a timeline outlining key milestones and deadlines for implementing your Facebook marketing plan.
- **Quarterly Reviews:** Schedule regular reviews to assess progress, adjust strategies, and set new goals.

- **Summary of Plan:** Recap the key elements of your Facebook marketing plan.
- **Call to Action:** Encourage team members to collaborate and execute the plan effectively.

Use this template as a framework to develop your Facebook marketing plan, customizing it to fit your business objectives, audience, and resources. Regularly review and update your plan to adapt to changes in your business environment and the evolving landscape of Facebook marketing.

Conclusion

A well-crafted Facebook marketing plan is essential for achieving your business objectives and maximizing your impact on the world's largest social media platform. Throughout this plan, we've outlined key strategies, tactics, and considerations to help you leverage Facebook effectively and drive meaningful results for your brand.

By setting clear goals and objectives, understanding your target audience, and developing a robust content and advertising strategy, you can position your brand for success on Facebook. Engaging with your audience authentically, leveraging user-generated content, and running targeted ad campaigns will help you build a loyal community and drive measurable outcomes.

Measurement and analytics play a crucial role in optimizing your Facebook marketing efforts. By regularly monitoring key metrics, tracking performance data, and iterating on your strategies based on insights, you can continuously improve your results and achieve greater ROI.

Remember that success on Facebook is not static; it requires ongoing effort, adaptation, and innovation. Stay informed about new features, trends, and best practices, and be prepared to adjust your approach as needed to stay ahead of the curve.

In implementing this Facebook marketing plan, we encourage collaboration, communication, and a commitment to excellence. Together, we can harness the power of Facebook to connect with our audience, drive engagement, and achieve our business objectives.

Thank you for your dedication and enthusiasm. Let's embark on this journey together and make a meaningful impact on Facebook and beyond.